CHETNA'S
EASY
BAKING

To my amazing kids, Sia and Yuv.

First published in Great Britain in 2022 by Hamlyn,
an imprint of Octopus Publishing Group Ltd,
Carmelite House, 50 Victoria Embankment, London EC4Y 0DZ
www.octopusbooks.co.uk
www.octopusbooksusa.com

An Hachette UK Company
www.hachette.co.uk

Design and layout copyright © Octopus Publishing Group 2022
Text copyright © Chetna Makan 2022

Distributed in the US by Hachette Book Group, 1290 Avenue of the Americas,
4th and 5th Floors, New York, NY 10104

Distributed in Canada by Canadian Manda Group, 664 Annette St., Toronto,
Ontario, Canada M6S 2C8

ISBN 978-0-60063-739-4

A CIP catalogue record for this book is available from the British Library.

Printed and bound in China.

10 9 8 7 6 5 4 3 2 1

Editorial Director: Eleanor Maxfield
Art Director: Juliette Norsworthy
Senior Editor: Pollyanna Poulter
Copy Editor: Lucy Bannell
Photographer: Nassima Rothacker
Food Stylist: Emily Kydd
Props Stylist: Morag Farquhar
Production: Lucy Carter and Nic Jones

CHETNA'S
EASY
BAKING

*with a twist
of spice*

CHETNA MAKAN

hamlyn

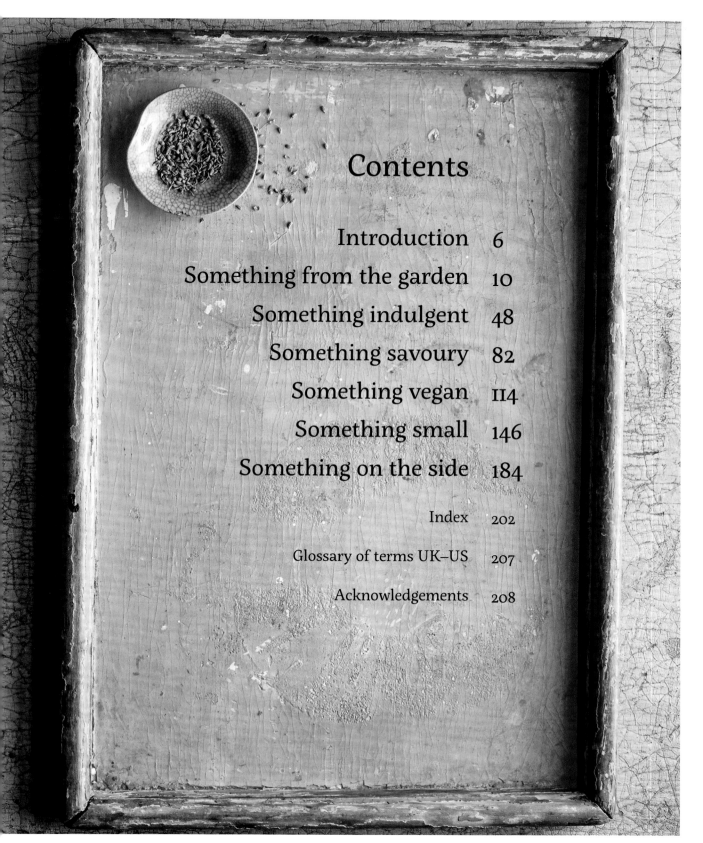

Contents

Introduction

I started baking young, but my clearest early memory of it is from when I was about 12 years old, the same age as my daughter is now, making my papa's birthday cake. It was just a simple vanilla sponge, but I had a torrid time trying to get the royal icing to set, not knowing what I was doing wrong or why it wouldn't harden up. I desperately wanted it to look amazing, as we were having a birthday party for papa.

Regardless of how the icing looked in the end – and I suspect it wasn't great – the cake was a success. Not because I mastered the royal icing, but because everyone gathered round and ate and smiled and celebrated together. That is the best thing about baking: creating something that will make your favourite people happy and give you the joy of sharing it. (I have since mastered royal icing, but you'll be relieved to know it doesn't appear in this book.) But that early experience also taught me something important: me and complicated bakes just don't go together.

I have always had a sweet tooth, inherited from my parents along with my love for all food. Growing up, I was surrounded by amazing Indian sweets, but I was lucky that my mum had a tiny round portable oven, something she still owns, just big enough to bake a cake (though its dimensions restricted the size of cake tin we could use). She was the only person we knew who owned an oven – of a curious kind I have never seen since – and she had a special love for baking cakes. Sometimes she would plug the oven in to bake in her room, sometimes in my room, and sometimes the oven would sit in the corridor, wafting out that distinctive cake-baking fragrance and making the whole house smell amazing. Her love of baking was passed directly to me. (My mum's famous date cake, which I featured in my very first book, remains the talk of her town. She still makes an egg-free version for her vegan friends.)

We had no cookbooks or internet to learn recipes or baking techniques from at the time, but there were cooking shows on telly and my mum would sit in front of those, taking notes. She also took a cookery course one summer in a lady's home, where she learned to

I want you to pick up this book and feel the confidence that you can do it, too.

make some cakes and ice creams. She still has those TV and cookery-course notebooks and I used them when I was learning to bake.

I started baking in my early teens and took it upon myself to bake birthday cakes for all five of us at home. They were not fancy multi-layered affairs, just simple sponges, sometimes with food colouring and sometimes with flavouring extracts added. I remember making a marble cake for the first time with half vanilla and half pink cake batter and being *very* pleased with the result!

Simple and inspiring

Throughout my baking life, one thing that has remained consistent is that love of simplicity. I have always preferred easy, rustic-looking food to pristine, too-pretty-to-eat bakes. There is something so warming and heartening about them, a quality that makes you enjoy eating them even more.

So that is the idea behind this, my sixth book. My very first book focused on baking and this is the only time I have revisited the subject since. And the reason why I've returned to baking is as simple as the bakes I love. Like all of us, I have spent a few months at home during the COVID-19 lockdowns, in my case watching my kids grow into teens and develop their love of food and cooking. My daughter Sia loves baking; if she can find the kitchen free (which doesn't happen often as I am always in there), she will be baking like a shot. She goes to my bookshelf, picks up a book, finds a recipe she wants to try and bakes it there and then.

Watching her do that made me want to write a baking book to inspire the young, the old and everyone in between, I want you to pick up this book and feel the confidence that you can do it, too.

Whether that's cooking up a glut of pears from your garden into a tarte Tatin spiced with star anise and studded with chocolate, creating an indulgent Masala Chai Tres Leches bake for a family occasion, or knocking up Potato Curry Puffs for a lunch you'll return to again and again, everyone can get involved

That is the best thing about baking: creating something that will make your favourite people happy and give you the joy of sharing it.

with these recipes. I've made sure to include a whole bunch of vegan-friendly bakes, too: try a cheesecake with a regal hint of saffron, tasty Peanut Masala Tear and Share Rolls to bring to a picnic, or simply the best chocolate cookies for a plant-based diet, lifted with cardamom and pistachios.

A baking inheritance: from me to you

The inspiration for every bake in this book comes from my own kitchen. These are recipes that I have been meaning to share for some time now, all simple bakes, with an added hint of spices from my Indian heritage. My hope is that this book is something you will keep for years to come, to inspire your children and – who knows? – perhaps your parents, too, to bring sweetness and joy into all your lives.

In this book, you will find a collection of simple sweet and savoury recipes, with ingredients that are easy to find, but which all contain something new to make your bakes sing and shine. That could be a spice you might not expect, a fusion of global influences that were just born to be together (Black Tahini Cheesecake Cookies, anyone?), or a twist on a classic, such as a drizzle cake dazzling with mango and ginger.

Most importantly, though, is that special ingredient that only you can bring to my book: that bit of love which you add to make every bake special.

Happy baking!

My hope is that this book is something you will keep for years to come, to inspire your children and – who knows? – perhaps your parents, too, to bring sweetness and joy into all your lives.

Something from the garden

Mango, ginger and lime cake

Pear, chocolate, star anise and hazelnut tarte Tatin

Gingered sweet potato traybake

Yogurt and white chocolate cake with passion fruit curd

Courgette and lemon cake

Rhubarb and custard crumble cake

Mango and lime meringue pie

Cherry, almond and honey upside-down cake

Banoffee chocolate pavlova

Raspberry and coconut cheesecake

Brownie meringue traybake with fresh berries

Pineapple elderflower cake

Beetroot, chocolate and coconut cake

Banana traybake with toffee-chocolate sauce

Kewra mango cake

As a mango lover, I want to make the most of mango season by not just eating as many mangoes as possible, but also baking with them. In this bundt cake, the flavours are very balanced and there is no one frontrunner. A variation of lemon drizzle cake, the sponge has lime and ginger running through it, while the mango gin syrup and icing gives a subtle mango zing. You can make this with mango juice instead of mango gin if you like, but if you like your gin, this is a must-try!

Mango, ginger and lime cake

SERVES 10–12

FOR THE CAKE

250g (9oz) unsalted butter, softened, plus more for the tin

250g (9oz) golden caster sugar

250g (9oz) self-raising flour

1 teaspoon baking powder

finely grated zest of 2 limes

5 large eggs

80g (2¾oz) stem ginger in syrup, finely chopped

FOR THE SYRUP

50g (1¾oz) caster sugar

70ml (2½fl oz) mango gin (I use Love Delhi Gin)

4 teaspoons syrup from the ginger jar

2 tablespoons water

FOR THE ICING

200g (7oz) icing sugar

50ml (1¾oz) mango gin

TO SERVE

40g (1½oz) stem ginger in syrup, finely chopped

1 mango, stoned, peeled and roughly chopped

Preheat the oven to 180°C (350°F), Gas Mark 4. Butter a 25cm (10 inch) bundt tin (mine is a 10-cup capacity tin).

Put all the cake ingredients apart from the stem ginger in the bowl of a food mixer fitted with the whisk attachment and beat for 2 minutes until fluffy and pale. Fold in the ginger. Pour the batter into the prepared tin and bake for 30–35 minutes until a skewer inserted comes out clean. Let it cool in the tin for 15 minutes.

Meanwhile, prepare the syrup by putting all the ingredients in a saucepan and bringing to the boil.

Remove the cake from the tin and, using a skewer, poke holes all over. Now brush the syrup over the cake, a little at a time, until it has all been absorbed. Let it cool completely.

Prepare the icing by mixing the icing sugar and gin until you have a slightly thick, but still spreadable, icing. Drizzle it all over the cake, sprinkle the ginger and mango on top and serve.

You can store this in an airtight container for 3–4 days.

Such a perfect way to end a meal: a flaky pastry base with soft pears, covered in star anise caramel, nuts and deep chocolate, served warm with ice cream or cream.

Pear, chocolate, star anise and hazelnut tarte Tatin

SERVES 6

320g (11¼oz) pack of ready-rolled puff pastry

70g (2½oz) unsalted butter

100g (3½oz) caster sugar

1 teaspoon ground star anise

4–6 pears, peeled, halved lengthways and cored

50g (1¾oz) roasted, chopped hazelnuts

50g (1¾oz) dark chocolate (70 per cent cocoa solids), roughly chopped

1 egg, lightly beaten

Before you start cooking, unroll the pastry. Take a 20–23cm (8–9 inch) ovenproof frying pan and cut out a circle of pastry the size of the pan. Place the pastry on a tray and put into the refrigerator until needed.

Preheat the oven to 180°C (350°F), Gas Mark 4.

Put the butter and sugar in the ovenproof frying pan and cook over a low heat for 5–6 minutes until caramelized. Add the star anise and stir.

Take the pan off the heat and place the pears, cut-sides up, on top of the caramel, keeping their narrow ends in the centre. Brush some of the caramel over the pears using a pastry brush. Bake for 30 minutes until the pears are soft.

Sprinkle the hazelnuts in the gaps between the pears, then scatter the chocolate on top of the nuts. Place the pastry circle on top and tuck it down around the pears. Using a knife, make cuts all over to let out some steam.

Brush it all over with some beaten egg and bake for 25–30 minutes until golden. Leave it for a minute before turning it out on to a plate. Slice and serve.

I am not a big fan of sweet potato in savoury dishes, I find it too sweet, but it works a treat in this recipe. It makes the cake moist, soft and delicious and you really can't tell there is sweet potato in there, which for me is a bonus. The ginger adds warmth to the sweet cake and a hint of lime gives freshness.

Gingered sweet potato traybake

SERVES 8–10

FOR THE CAKE

2 sweet potatoes

200ml (7fl oz) rapeseed oil, plus more for the sweet potatoes and the tin

200g (7oz) self-raising flour

½ teaspoon baking powder

½ teaspoon bicarbonate of soda

½ teaspoon fine sea salt

250g (9oz) soft light brown sugar

1 teaspoon ground ginger

3 large eggs

100g (3½oz) pecans, roughly chopped

finely grated zest of 1 lime

50g (1¾oz) stem ginger in syrup, finely chopped

FOR THE ICING

300g (10½oz) full-fat cream cheese

3 tablespoons soft light brown sugar

finely grated zest of 1 lime, plus extra to decorate

handful of pecans, roughly chopped

Preheat the oven to 200°C (400°F), Gas Mark 6. Prick the potatoes all over with a sharp knife, then oil them and place them on a baking tray lined with foil. Bake for 50 minutes until softened, then set aside to cool. Once cooled, peel the potatoes and mash the flesh with a fork, you need roughly 200g (7oz) of pulp in total.

Oil a 30 x 20cm (12 x 8 inch) cake tin and line it with nonstick baking paper. Reduce the oven temperature to 180°C (350°F), Gas Mark 4.

In a bowl, combine all the dry ingredients for the cake and mix well. Add the oil and eggs and whisk with an electric whisk for 1 minute. Then add the sweet potato pulp and whisk for another minute until creamy and smooth. Fold in the pecans, lime zest and stem ginger.

Pour the batter into the prepared tin and bake for 35–40 minutes until a skewer inserted comes out clean. Leave it to cool in the tin for 10 minutes, then turn out on to a wire rack.

In a bowl, combine the cream cheese with the sugar and lime zest and spread over the cooled cake. Sprinkle the pecans and extra lime zest on top and serve.

You can store this in an airtight container in the refrigerator for 3–4 days. Bring it to room temperature before serving.

I am a big fan of no-fuss, simple yet stunning cakes and this one surely comes in that category. The lemon zest with the passion fruit curd swirled into the white chocolate batter is sublime. Yogurt makes this cake moist and light and all it needs is a sprinkling of some icing sugar to finish.

Yogurt and white chocolate cake with passion fruit curd

SERVES 8–10

125g (4½oz) unsalted butter, softened, plus more for the tin

125g (4½oz) caster sugar

2 large eggs

finely grated zest of 2 lemons

125g (4½oz) natural yogurt

220g (7¾oz) self-raising flour

100g (3½oz) white chocolate, melted

6 tablespoons Lemon and passion fruit curd (see page 188)

icing sugar, to finish

Preheat the oven to 180°C (350°F), Gas Mark 4. Butter a 20cm (8 inch) round cake tin and line with nonstick baking paper.

Put the butter and sugar in a bowl and whisk with an electric whisk for 2 minutes until creamy and pale. Next, add the eggs, lemon zest, yogurt, flour and melted chocolate and whisk for 2 minutes until fluffy and smooth.

Pour the mix into the prepared tin and add the 6 tablespoons of curd in separate fairly evenly spaced dollops. Using a skewer, swirl it roughly into the batter.

Bake for 55–60 minutes until a skewer inserted comes out clean.

Let it cool in the tin for 10 minutes before taking it out. Sprinkle icing sugar on top and serve warm or at room temperature.

This can be stored in an airtight container for 3–4 days.

A cake that screams summer, to be enjoyed with afternoon tea or after a lovely barbecue. Light, spongy, fresh with lemon and with an extra hit from lemon liqueur. The courgette just adds to the texture and makes the cake super-moist, the syrup ensures it doesn't dry out and the cream cheese adds a subtle creamy touch.

Courgette and lemon cake

SERVES 10–12

FOR THE CAKE

200ml (7fl oz) sunflower oil

200g (7oz) golden caster sugar

4 large eggs

finely grated zest and juice of 1 lemon, plus extra zest to decorate

250g (9oz) self-raising flour

1 teaspoon bicarbonate of soda

1 courgette, roughly 250g (9oz), grated

FOR THE SYRUP

50g (1¾oz) caster sugar

50ml (1¾fl oz) water

2 tablespoons limoncello

FOR THE ICING

300g (10½oz) full-fat cream cheese

50g (1¾oz) icing sugar

Preheat the oven to 180°C (350°F), Gas Mark 4. Oil 2 x 20cm (8 inch) round cake tins and line the bases with nonstick baking paper.

In a large bowl, combine the oil, sugar and eggs and beat with an electric whisk for 2 minutes until fluffy. Add the lemon zest and juice, flour, bicarbonate of soda and courgette. Fold it all in well and divide the mixture equally between the prepared tins.

Bake for 35–40 minutes until a skewer inserted comes out clean. Let the cakes cool completely.

In a saucepan, boil the sugar, measured water and limoncello together until the sugar has dissolved, then let it cool slightly. Brush this over the warm cakes and let them cool completely.

Put the cream cheese and icing sugar in a bowl and mix until smooth. Spread half over one cake and place the second cake on top. Spread the rest of the cream cheese over the cake, sprinkle with the extra lemon zest and serve.

You can store this in an airtight container in the refrigerator for 3–4 days. Bring it to room temperature before serving.

You don't get rhubarb in India. The first time I tasted it, it reminded me of an Indian fruit called karonda because of its tart and sour taste... and since I love karonda, I love rhubarb too. Rhubarb and custard is a classic combination. I have tried to combine them in such a way that the cake remains moist and you find a little rhubarb and custard in every other bite. The crumble just adds another texture, as well as warmth from the ginger. Enjoy it warm with ice cream, or pour warm custard over the cold cake. The choice is yours.

Rhubarb and custard crumble cake

SERVES 10–12

FOR THE CAKE

250g (9oz) unsalted butter, softened, plus more for the tin

250g (9oz) golden caster sugar

4 large eggs

250g (9oz) self-raising flour

1 teaspoon baking powder

1 teaspoon ground ginger

8 tablespoons ready-made custard

200g (7oz) rhubarb, cut into 1cm (½ inch) pieces

FOR THE CRUMBLE

100g (3½oz) plain flour

1 tablespoon golden caster sugar

½ teaspoon ground ginger

Preheat the oven to 180°C (350°F), Gas Mark 4. Butter a 25cm (10 inch) round cake tin and line the base with nonstick baking paper.

In a bowl, whisk the butter and sugar for 2 minutes with an electric whisk until creamy and pale. You can also use a food mixer fitted with the paddle attachment for this. Now add the eggs and whisk for a few seconds. Next, add the flour, baking powder, ginger and 3 tablespoons of the custard and whisk for a minute until the mixture is well combined and fluffy.

Put 100g (3½oz) of the batter in another bowl. Add the rhubarb to the big bowl of batter and fold in. Pour this into the prepared tin. With the back of a spoon, make 5 hollows in the batter and pour 1 tablespoon of custard into each.

Now prepare the crumble. Add the flour, sugar and ginger to the reserved batter and rub in gently. Sprinkle over the batter in the tin, then bake for 55–60 minutes until a skewer inserted comes out clean.

Leave the cake in the tin for 10 minutes before taking it out. Serve it warm or at room temperature.

You can store this in an airtight container for 3–4 days.

Mango, my favourite fruit, is the star of this recipe. I discovered lemon meringue pie when I moved to the UK many years ago and the combination of short pastry, sharp filling and light-as-air sweet meringue made me fall in love with it. This recipe combines my favourite fruit and one of my favourite desserts into one, resulting in this sublime beauty.

Mango and lime meringue pie

SERVES 10–12

FOR THE PASTRY

200g (7oz) plain flour, plus more for dusting

20g (¾oz) golden caster sugar

100g (3½oz) unsalted butter, chilled and chopped into small cubes

1 large egg, lightly beaten

1 teaspoon lemon juice

FOR THE MANGO AND LIME CURD

150g (5½oz) mango purée

finely grated zest and juice of 2 limes

180g (6¼oz) caster sugar

50g (1¾oz) unsalted butter

2 tablespoons cornflour

4 large eggs, plus 4 large egg yolks

FOR THE MERINGUE

4 egg whites

200g (7oz) caster sugar

1 tablespoon cornflour

To make the pastry, mix the flour and sugar in a large bowl. Add the butter and coat it with the flour. Use your fingertips to rub the butter into the flour until the mixture looks like crumbs.

Mix the egg and lemon juice together and pour in just enough of this liquid to bring the dough together. You might not need it all.

Gently knead the dough on a lightly floured surface for a few seconds, then shape into a ball. Wrap in clingfilm and rest in the refrigerator for 10–15 minutes.

Preheat the oven to 180°C (350°F), Gas Mark 4. On a floured surface, roll out the pastry to a circle, 5mm (¼ inch) thick. Line a 23cm (9 inch) loose-bottomed tart tin with the pastry, leaving the excess hanging over the edge, and prick the base all over with a fork.

Scrunch up some nonstick baking paper, then unscrunch it, put it in the tin and fill with baking beans. Blind-bake for 15 minutes, then remove the paper and the beans and bake for a further 20 minutes or until the pastry looks dry and crisp. Use a small sharp knife to trim the excess pastry from the rim.

continued overleaf

To prepare the mango and lime curd, mix the mango purée, lime zest and juice, sugar, butter and cornflour in a saucepan and bring it to the boil, stirring until the sugar has dissolved. In a bowl, whisk the eggs and egg yolks together, then slowly add this to the pan of mango mixture. Cook over a low heat for 8–10 minutes until the mixture thickens, stirring continuously. Sieve it into a clean bowl, then pour it into the pastry case.

In a clean bowl, beat the egg whites with an electric whisk until they form soft peaks, then slowly add the sugar bit by bit, continuing to whisk. Add the cornflour and whisk for a couple of minutes until the mix is smooth, shiny and stiff. Spread this over the mango and lime curd and make some swirls in the meringue with the back of a spoon.

Bake for 15–20 minutes until the meringue is lightly golden and crisp.

Let it cool completely in the tart case. Serve it on the day it was baked.

Living in Kent I am very lucky to have an abundance of cherries in the season and as much as I like to enjoy them as is, they are great in bakes too. This very delicately flavoured cake is a crowd-pleaser. Not only is it easy to make, it also somehow tastes of long summer evenings. Enjoy warm with a scoop of ice cream, or serve with some crème fraîche.

Cherry, almond and honey upside-down cake

SERVES 10–12

220g (7¾oz) unsalted butter, softened, plus more for the tin

250g (9oz) cherries, halved

70g (2½oz) flaked almonds

200g (7oz) runny honey, plus 2–3 tablespoons, to glaze

100g (3½oz) golden caster sugar

100g (3½oz) ground almonds

120g (4¼oz) self-raising flour

4 large eggs

Preheat the oven to 180°C (350°F), Gas Mark 4. Butter a 25cm (10 inch) springform round cake tin and line the base with nonstick baking paper. Place the cherries, cut-sides down, in the prepared tin. Sprinkle some of the flaked almonds in between the cherries.

Put all the ingredients for the cake, except for the remaining flaked almonds, in a bowl and whisk for 2 minutes with an electric whisk until the batter is creamy and fluffy. You can also use a food mixer fitted with the paddle attachment. Now add the rest of the flaked almonds and fold them in. Pour the batter into the prepared tin and bake for 40–45 minutes until a skewer inserted comes out clean.

Let the cake sit in the tin for 5 minutes, then turn it out onto a plate and carefully peel off the baking paper.

Warm the 2–3 tablespoons honey until it's runny and spreadable and brush this over the cherries.

This will keep in an airtight container in the refrigerator for 3–4 days. Bring it to room temperature before serving.

Banana and toffee is a combination you really can't say no to, especially if it is served on a chocolate-flavoured meringue. The crisp meringue with the fresh cream, buttery bananas and caramel sauce... this dessert disappears in seconds once it hits the table in our house.

Banoffee chocolate pavlova

SERVES 8

FOR THE MERINGUE

4 egg whites

200g (7oz) caster sugar

1 teaspoon cornflour

100g (3½oz) dark chocolate (70 per cent cocoa solids), melted and slightly cooled

FOR THE TOPPING

3 tablespoons unsalted butter

4 bananas, peeled and halved lengthways

4–6 tablespoons Salted caramel sauce (see page 189)

500ml (18fl oz) double cream

2 tablespoons caster sugar

Preheat the oven to 120°C (250°F), Gas Mark ½. Line a baking tray with nonstick baking paper. Draw a 20cm (8 inch) circle on the paper and turn it over, so the pencil mark is on the bottom but still visible.

In a bowl, whisk the egg whites with an electric whisk until they form soft peaks, then add the caster sugar 1 tablespoon at a time and whisk until combined. Now add the cornflour and whisk until the mixture is glossy and stiff. Drizzle the cooled melted chocolate all over and, without mixing too much, scoop out the meringue.

Spread it on the prepared tray within the circle in the shape of a crater, with the sides a little higher than the middle. Bake for 1½ hours until crispy and dried out. Set aside to cool.

Heat the butter in a saucepan and cook the bananas for 2–3 minutes until caramelized on both sides. Set aside to cool.

Once you are ready to serve, whip the cream with the sugar with an electric whisk until it forms soft peaks. Place the meringue on a serving plate and spoon over the cream. Top with the caramelized bananas, drizzle over the caramel sauce and serve immediately.

There is something about the simplicity of a baked cheesecake with its rich texture and flavour that makes it perfect for a gathering. The addition of coconut cream here gives lightness, while the raspberries in turn cut through the cream cheese. The caramel sauce is purely there because I am greedy and have a massive sweet tooth. You can of course serve it without the sauce if you prefer.

Raspberry and coconut cheesecake

SERVES 8–10

75g (2¾oz) unsalted butter, melted, plus more for the tin

250g (9oz) chocolate digestive biscuits

450g (1lb) full-fat cream cheese

140g (5oz) caster sugar

½ teaspoon fine sea salt

300g (10½oz) coconut cream

150g (5½oz) soured cream

3 large eggs, lightly beaten

200g (7oz) raspberries

½ quantity Salted caramel sauce (see page 189)

Preheat the oven to 180°C (350°F), Gas Mark 4. Butter a 20cm (8 inch) springform round cake tin and line the base with nonstick baking paper.

Put the biscuits in a ziplock bag and crush with a rolling pin. Place the crushed biscuits and melted butter in a bowl and mix well. Put in the prepared tin and press down so it's nicely compressed. Place the tin on a baking tray and bake for 15 minutes.

Meanwhile, prepare the filling. Put the cream cheese and sugar in a bowl and whisk with an electric whisk until smooth. Now add the salt, coconut cream, soured cream and eggs and whisk it all together. Add half the raspberries and fold them in. Pour this on to the biscuit base. Bake for around 1 hour until only the centre of the cheesecake is wobbly. Turn off the oven but leave the cheesecake inside, door slightly ajar, to continue cooking for another 30 minutes. Remove from the oven and leave in the tin to cool completely. Chill thoroughly, overnight if possible.

Remove the cheesecake from the tin and place it on a serving plate. Drizzle the caramel sauce on top, scatter over the remaining raspberries and serve.

Any leftovers can be stored in an airtight container in the refrigerator for 3–4 days.

This is purely the result of putting all the things my kids like in one bake. They love brownies, meringue, cream and berries and that is how this came about. It's safe to say that they absolutely love this.

SERVES 10–12

FOR THE BROWNIE

300g (10½oz) unsalted butter, plus more for the tin

300g (10½oz) dark chocolate (70 per cent cocoa solids)

5 large eggs

300g (10½oz) golden caster sugar

pinch of fine sea salt

1 teaspoon vanilla extract

150g (5½oz) plain flour

50g (1¾oz) cocoa powder

50g (1¾oz) pistachios, finely chopped

FOR THE MERINGUE

4 egg whites

200g (7oz) golden caster sugar

1 teaspoon cornflour

TO SERVE

50g (1¾oz) pistachios, finely chopped

300g (10½oz) double cream

2 tablespoons caster sugar

300g (10½oz) mixed berries, such as strawberries, raspberries and blueberries

Brownie meringue traybake with fresh berries

Preheat the oven to 180°C (350°F), Gas Mark 4. Butter a 30 x 20cm (12 x 8 inch) rectangular tin and then line the base with nonstick baking paper.

Start with the brownies. Put the chocolate and butter in a heatproof bowl set over a saucepan of simmering water. Stir until melted, then set aside to cool slightly.

In a separate bowl, whisk the eggs and sugar with an electric whisk for 6 minutes until creamy and pale. Add the melted chocolate mixture and whisk for a few seconds to combine. Add the rest of the ingredients and fold in, then pour the batter into the prepared tin.

Now for the meringue. In a clean bowl, whisk the egg whites with an electric whisk until they form soft peaks. Add the sugar 1 tablespoon at a time and continue to whisk until combined. Add the cornflour and whisk for 1–2 minutes until glossy and stiff. Pour this over the brownie mix and spread it out evenly.

Sprinkle most of the pistachios on top and bake for 35 minutes until the meringue looks golden. Set aside to cool completely.

Whip the cream and sugar in a bowl until soft peaks form. Dollop this over the meringue. Scatter over the berries and the reserved pistachios and serve immediately.

I have a soft spot for pineapple cake. It was the most popular cake at the bakeries in Jabalpur: a light, eggless sponge with fresh cream and pineapple on top. I have tried to make it at home but it's not the same. As with many ingredients, the cream in the UK tastes different to the cream you get in India. So I have made my own version, adding the pineapple to the cake and, since I have elderflower in my garden, I have incorporated it here to lend a summery, floral note. It's so light and refreshing that you might find it serves far fewer people than I say!

Pineapple elderflower cake

SERVES 8–10

FOR THE CAKE

100g (3½oz) unsalted butter, softened, plus more for the tin

220g (7¾oz) canned pineapple pieces, roughly chopped

200g (7oz) caster sugar

100g (3½oz) ground almonds

100g (3½oz) self-raising flour

½ teaspoon bicarbonate of soda

3 large eggs

130g (4¾oz) natural yogurt

2 tablespoons elderflower cordial

FOR THE CREAM

300ml (½ pint) double cream

30g (1oz) caster sugar

1 tablespoon elderflower cordial

elderflowers, to decorate (optional)

Preheat the oven to 180°C (350°F), Gas Mark 4. Butter 2 x 20cm (8 inch) round cake tins and line the bases with nonstick baking paper. Scatter half the pineapple over one tin.

In a large bowl, with an electric whisk, or in a food mixer fitted with the paddle attachment, put all the cake ingredients except the remaining pineapple and whisk for a minute until smooth and pale. Stir in the remaining pineapple pieces. Divide the batter equally between the prepared tins and bake for 35 minutes or until a skewer inserted comes out clean. Set aside to cool completely.

Whip the cream, sugar and elderflower cordial together in a bowl with an electric whisk until it forms soft peaks.

Put the cake without pineapple on top of a serving plate and spread all the cream on top. Place the second cake, pineapple-side up, on top. If you manage to find some elderflowers, place on top of the cake and serve.

This cake can be stored in an airtight container in the refrigerator for 3–4 days. Bring it to room temperature before serving.

When in doubt, make a chocolate cake. This is also packed with gorgeous beetroot which gives it softness and bounce and coconut which adds a creamy feel. Making the ganache with coconut milk allows the coconut flavour to shine.

Beetroot, chocolate and coconut cake

SERVES 10–12

FOR THE CAKE

100ml (3½fl oz) rapeseed oil, plus more for the tin

250g (9oz) dark chocolate (70 per cent cocoa solids)

100g (3½oz) self-raising flour

½ teaspoon baking powder

½ teaspoon bicarbonate of soda

50g (1¾oz) ground almonds

1 tablespoon cocoa powder

50g (1¾oz) desiccated coconut

200g (7oz) soft brown sugar

3 large eggs

250g (9oz) raw beetroot, grated

1 teaspoon vanilla extract

FOR THE GANACHE

400ml (14fl oz) can of good-quality full-fat coconut milk

200g (7oz) dark chocolate (70 per cent cocoa solids), roughly chopped

Preheat the oven to 180°C (350°F), Gas Mark 4. Oil a 25cm (10 inch) round cake tin and line it with nonstick baking paper.

Start with the cake. Break the chocolate into a heatproof bowl and set it over a saucepan of simmering water until melted (make sure the bowl does not touch the water). Set aside to cool slightly.

In a bowl, combine the flour, baking powder, bicarbonate of soda, ground almonds, cocoa and coconut and mix well. In a separate large bowl, whisk the oil and sugar for a minute with an electric whisk until smooth. Add the eggs and whisk until combined.

Add the melted chocolate and beetroot to the cake batter with the vanilla and mix well. Now add the dry ingredients and fold them all in, making sure everything is mixed well.

Pour the cake batter into the prepared tin and bake for 55–60 minutes until a skewer inserted comes out clean. Leave the cake to cool in the tin for 10 minutes, then turn it out and place on a wire rack.

Meanwhile, prepare the ganache. Without shaking the can of coconut milk, open it, scoop out the solids and add them to a saucepan. Heat until they start to bubble. Put the chocolate in a heatproof bowl, pour the hot coconut milk on top and stir until the chocolate melts.

Once the cake has cooled, transfer it to a serving plate, pour the ganache on top and serve warm, or wait until the ganache has set slightly.

Store in an airtight container in the refrigerator for 3–4 days. You might want to warm the slices in the microwave for 10 seconds before serving.

I am not a big fan of banana breads as I find them dry and mostly a bit boring. So, I made this cake a couple of years ago to tick all the boxes with taste, texture and looks and it was an instant hit with my family. The kids love it warm as it is and if we have any left over, they always warm it in the microwave for 10 seconds before eating.

Banana traybake with toffee-chocolate sauce

SERVES 10–12

FOR THE CAKE

200g (7oz) unsalted butter, softened, plus more for the tin

200g (7oz) light soft brown sugar

1 teaspoon vanilla extract

4 large eggs

½ teaspoon baking powder

250g (9oz) self-raising flour

60g (2¼oz) natural yogurt

100g (3½oz) dark chocolate (70 per cent cocoa solids), roughly chopped

50g (1¾oz) pecan nuts, roughly chopped

2 ripe bananas, peeled and mashed with a fork

FOR THE SAUCE

50g (1¾oz) unsalted butter

100g (3½oz) dark soft brown sugar

150ml (5fl oz) double cream

pinch of salt

1 tablespoon golden syrup

50g (1¾oz) dark chocolate (70 per cent cocoa solids), roughly chopped

Preheat the oven to 180°C (350°F), Gas Mark 4. Butter a 30 x 20 x 4–5cm (12 x 8 x 2 inch) traybake tin and line it with nonstick baking paper.

In a bowl, beat the butter and light soft brown sugar with an electric whisk for 2 minutes until creamy and pale. Now add the vanilla and eggs and mix for a few more seconds. Next, add the rest of the ingredients and combine well. Pour this into the prepared tin and bake for 35 minutes until a skewer inserted comes out clean. Leave to cool in the tray for 10 minutes.

Meanwhile, prepare the sauce. In a saucepan over a medium-low heat, combine the butter, sugar, cream and salt and stir until the sugar has dissolved. Add the golden syrup and let it simmer for 2 minutes. Take it off the heat and let it sit for 2 minutes.

Now add the chocolate to the syrup mixture and stir until the chocolate has melted. Pour this over the cake and serve.

Store the cake in an airtight container for 3–4 days.

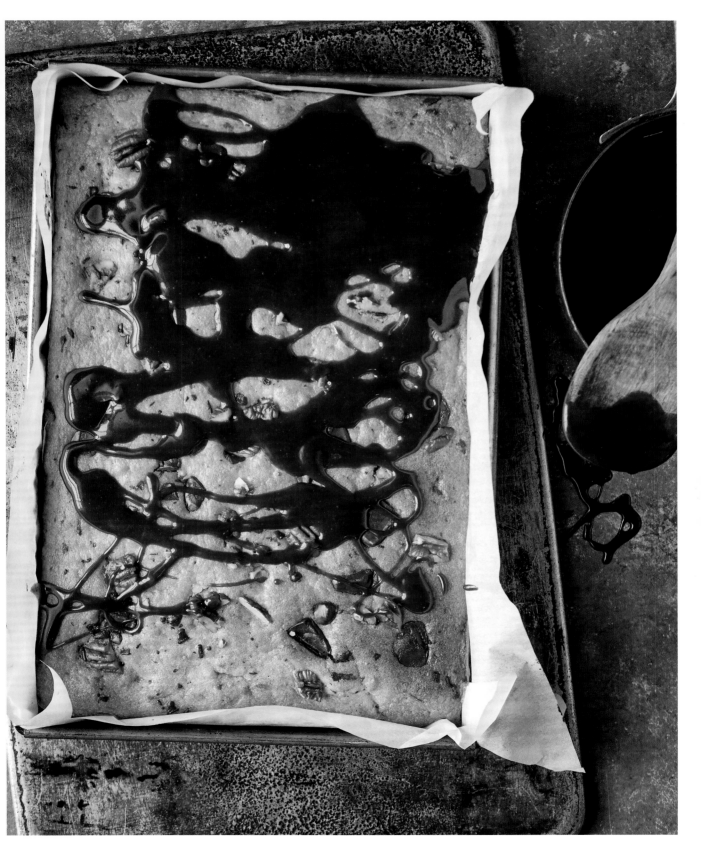

Kewra water is a fragrant extract made from pandanus flowers. It can smell similar to rosewater and it always reminds me of the refreshing Indian drink called khus sharbat, which is just amazing. A bottle of kewra water was always lingering in my family's kitchen cupboards, as it's often used in rice dishes, especially biryani, and also in some sweets. You can buy it in subcontinental shops, and online, of course. Here I combine it with my favourite fruit, mango, to make what I consider one of the most delicious cakes in this book.

Kewra mango cake

SERVES 8–10

FOR THE CAKE

200g (7oz) unsalted butter, softened, plus more for the tin

200g (7oz) caster sugar

4 large eggs

200g (7oz) self-raising flour

1 teaspoon baking powder

2 teaspoons kewra water

100g (3½oz) pistachios, roughly ground, plus more to serve

FOR THE FILLING

500ml (18fl oz) double cream

3 tablespoons caster sugar

2 ripe mangoes, stoned, peeled and roughly chopped

Preheat the oven to 180°C (350°F), Gas Mark 4. Butter and line 2 x 20cm (8 inch) round cake tins and line the bases with nonstick baking paper.

Put the butter, sugar, eggs, flour and baking powder in a bowl and whisk for 2 minutes with an electric whisk until pale and fluffy. Now add the kewra water and the pistachios and whisk for a few seconds until everything is well combined.

Divide the batter evenly between the prepared tins and bake for 30–35 minutes until a skewer inserted comes out clean. Leave the cakes to cool in the tins for 10 minutes, before turning out on to a wire rack to cool completely.

In a bowl, whip the cream and sugar until it forms soft peaks. Now add half the mango and fold it in.

Place one cake on a serving plate, spoon on half the cream and spread it out evenly. Place the second cake on top and spread over the rest of the cream. Now arrange the rest of the mango on top, sprinkle with pistachios and serve.

This is best enjoyed fresh, but any leftovers can be stored in the refrigerator for 3–4 days. Bring it to room temperature before serving.

Something indulgent

Masala chai tres leches cake

Cardamom and walnut sticky
toffee pudding

Black tahini honey tart

Saffron fennel loaf cake

Rose, coffee and chocolate tiramisu

Brownie pecan tart

Nutty frangipane filo tart

Chocolate and coconut spiced
self-saucing pudding

Rose and cardamom cheesecake

Orange and cinnamon savarin

Almond and caramel torte with
chocolate buttercream

Walnut and date swirl bread

Almond and cardamom custard cake

Here I have combined one of my favourite cakes with one of my favourite flavours. I was introduced to tres leches cake at a local cake club; they met once a month, chose a theme and everyone baked something that worked with the theme. After I took part in *Bake Off* the group invited me to a meeting and the members had all made cakes from different parts of the world. That was the first time I tried tres leches cake; I fell in love with it straight away. I think I have done justice to it with this masala chai infusion.

Masala chai tres leches cake

SERVES 12–14

FOR THE CAKE

unsalted butter, for the tin

6 large eggs, separated

200g (7oz) caster sugar

250g (9oz) plain flour

1½ teaspoons baking powder

1 teaspoon ground ginger

1 teaspoon ground cardamom

1 teaspoon ground cinnamon

½ teaspoon ground cloves

100ml (3½fl oz) whole milk

FOR THE SOAK

397g (13½oz) can of condensed milk

410g (14¼oz) can of evaporated milk

200ml (7fl oz) double cream

4 teabags

TO DECORATE

500ml (18fl oz) double cream

1 tablespoon caster sugar

½ teaspoon ground cinnamon

Preheat the oven to 180°C (350°F), Gas Mark 4. Butter a 30 x 20 x 4–5cm (12 x 8 x 2 inch) traybake tin and line it with nonstick baking paper.

In a bowl and using an electric whisk, beat the egg yolks with half the sugar for 5–6 minutes until pale, fluffy and almost doubled in size. In a separate bowl, combine the flour, baking powder and spices and mix well. Add the dry ingredients to the egg yolk mixture and fold them in, then gently fold in the milk as well.

In another bowl, beat the egg whites with a clean electric whisk until they have formed soft peaks. Slowly add the remaining sugar, 1 tablespoon at a time, whisking constantly. Once it is stiff and glossy, add a ladle of it to the batter and fold it in. Now add all the remaining egg whites and fold them in gently. Pour this mixture into the prepared tin, spreading it out evenly, and bake for 30 minutes until a skewer inserted comes out clean.

Meanwhile, combine all the soak ingredients in a saucepan and bring to the boil. Set aside to cool and infuse while the cake is baking.

continued overleaf

Once the cake is baked, immediately use a toothpick or skewer to prick all over the top. Remove the teabags from the saucepan and pour all the liquid evenly over the cake. Leave it to cool completely, then chill for 3–4 hours, or overnight, if possible.

To serve, whip the cream with the sugar until thickened and smooth. Top portions of the cake with the cream, a sprinkling of cinnamon and a drizzle of the soak from the tin.

Store in an airtight container in the refrigerator for 3–4 days.

If I see a sticky toffee pudding on a menu in a restaurant I have to order it. As easy as it is to make, it is really much sweeter than any other cake, so you have to be careful to get the flavour right. Here there is a lovely balance, with the cardamom in the sauce beautifully complementing the nuttiness of the walnuts.

Cardamom and walnut sticky toffee pudding

SERVES 10–12

FOR THE CAKE

220g (8oz) mejdool dates, pitted and roughly chopped

220ml (8fl oz) boiling water

80g (2¾oz) unsalted butter, softened, plus more for the tin

60g (2¼oz) dark soft brown sugar

2 tablespoons black treacle

2 large eggs

150g (5½oz) plain flour

1 teaspoon baking powder

1 teaspoon bicarbonate of soda

100g (3½oz) walnuts, finely chopped

FOR THE SAUCE

80g (2¾oz) salted butter, cut into cubes

150g (5½oz) dark soft brown sugar

1 tablespoon black treacle

1 teaspoon ground cardamom

220ml (8fl oz) double cream

Put the dates in a bowl with the measured water and let sit for 30 minutes. Use a fork to mash the softened dates into the liquid.

Preheat the oven to 180°C (350°F), Gas Mark 4. Butter a 20cm (8 inch) square loose-bottomed cake tin.

In a bowl, whisk the butter and dark soft brown sugar with an electric whisk for a minute until it turns paler. Spoon in the treacle and whisk for a few seconds until combined. Add the eggs and whisk again. Tip in the flour, baking powder, bicarbonate of soda and walnuts, then pour in the mushy date liquid and fold it all in.

Pour the cake batter into the prepared tin and bake for 35 minutes, or until a skewer inserted comes out clean.

Meanwhile, prepare the sauce. Heat the butter and sugar in a saucepan for a few minutes until the sugar has dissolved. Stir in the treacle and cardamom, then pour in the cream and continue to stir until combined. Let it bubble for a minute, then take it off the heat.

As soon as the cake is baked, use a skewer to make holes all over the cake. Pour half the sauce evenly over the cake and let it sit for 30 minutes before serving.

Serve with the remaining sauce, or some double cream or ice cream, the choice is yours.

Any leftovers can be kept in the refrigerator. Warm portions in a microwave on high for 15–20 seconds before serving.

Sesame seeds are used a lot in Indian food, especially sweets, sometimes ground to a paste. I recently found some black sesame paste and decided to make this tart. Dramatic and moody to look at, I'm sure there will be many questions when you serve it. Hopefully the earthiness of the tahini with the sweetness of the honey and the buttery short pastry will go down well. It's a dream team right here.

Black tahini honey tart

SERVES 10–12

FOR THE PASTRY

100g (3½oz) unsalted butter, softened

30g (1oz) tahini

30g (1oz) icing sugar

pinch of salt

2 egg yolks

200g (7oz) plain flour, plus more for dusting

FOR THE FILLING

180g (6½oz) unsalted butter

200g (7oz) honey

100g (3½oz) light soft brown sugar

3 large eggs, plus 2 large egg yolks, lightly beaten

125ml (4fl oz) double cream

2 tablespoons black tahini

1 teaspoon cider vinegar

pinch of salt

2 tablespoons black sesame seeds

To make the pastry, combine the butter, tahini, icing sugar and salt in a bowl. Mix with a wooden spoon until creamy and smooth. Add the egg yolks and mix again. Fold in the flour. Add 1–2 tablespoons water to bring the dough together. Press the dough into a circle, wrap in clingfilm and refrigerate for 2–3 hours.

Roll out the pastry on a lightly floured surface to a 2–3mm- ($1/8$ inch-) thick circle big enough to line a 20cm (8 inch) tart tin. You should have 1–2.5cm (½–1 inch) extra hanging over the tin. Line the tin with the pastry. Let it rest in the refrigerator for 30 minutes.

Preheat the oven to 180°C (350°F), Gas Mark 4. Prick the base of the tart with a fork. Scrunch up some nonstick baking paper, then unscrunch it, put it in the tin and fill with baking beans. Blind-bake for 15 minutes. Remove the paper and beans and bake for a further 15 minutes until golden. After 10 minutes, cut off the excess pastry.

Meanwhile, prepare the filling by heating the butter in a saucepan until it starts to bubble and change colour and the milk solids start to turn golden. Transfer to a bowl, and, once it is slightly cool, add the rest of the filling ingredients except the sesame seeds. Whisk it well and then pour this carefully into the tart case.

Sprinkle with sesame seeds and bake for 50–55 minutes until the filling has puffed up and is golden with a slight wobble in the middle. Let it cool completely, then remove from the tin and serve.

Best eaten the day you make it, after that the pastry starts to soften.

Saffron is such a special ingredient for me as it reminds me of festivals and feasts enjoyed with my family in India. It is used in celebratory biryani or kheer, to make the food special. I love cakes and sometimes I just want a good hearty sponge with no frills and this recipe is perfect in every sense. The subtle saffron makes the cake glow, with fennel lending its aniseed tone. Finished with a hint of lemon, this cake is simply stunning.

Saffron fennel loaf cake

SERVES 8–10

FOR THE CAKE

200g (7oz) unsalted butter, softened, plus more for the tin

big pinch of saffron threads

2 tablespoons warm whole milk

1½ tablespoons fennel seeds

200g (7oz) caster sugar

200g (7oz) self-raising flour

1 teaspoon baking powder

3 large eggs

2 tablespoons soured cream

pinch of fine sea salt

FOR THE ICING

50g (1¾oz) icing sugar

2 teaspoons lemon juice

Preheat the oven to 180°C (350°F), Gas Mark 4. Butter and line a 900g (2lb) loaf tin.

Put the saffron in a small bowl, pour the warm milk on top and let it infuse for 2 minutes. In a dry frying pan, toast the fennel seeds over a low heat for a minute until they release their aroma. Crush them in a mortar and pestle to break them up.

Put the butter and sugar in a bowl and beat with an electric whisk, or use a stand mixer fitted with the paddle attachment, for a couple of minutes until creamy and pale. Now add the rest of the cake ingredients, except the saffron mixture and fennel seeds, to the bowl and whisk for a minute. Lastly, add the saffron-infused milk and 1 tablespoon of the crushed fennel seeds and whisk for a few seconds. Pour the mixture into the prepared tin and bake for 1 hour–1 hour 5 minutes until a skewer inserted comes out clean. Let it cool in the cake tin for 10 minutes before removing.

Combine the icing sugar and lemon juice in a small bowl. Put the cake on a serving plate and drizzle the icing on top. Sprinkle with the remaining toasted fennel seeds and serve.

Store in an airtight container for 3–4 days.

Tiramisu is my son's absolute favourite dessert. Over the years, I have made this for my kids' birthday puddings and also adapted it into a cake for their birthdays. Once, an Italian friend of mine, Giulia, told me that the tiramisu I made for her was just like the recipe she grew up with. That was all I needed to hear. I have added an extra layer of chocolate and a floral touch to the cream; the result is just dreamy.

Rose, coffee and chocolate tiramisu

SERVES 10–12

4 large eggs, separated

100g (3½oz) caster sugar

2 teaspoons rosewater

250g (9oz) mascarpone cheese

450ml (16fl oz) double cream

4 tablespoons instant coffee granules

400ml (14fl oz) boiling water

3 tablespoons coffee liqueur

350g (12oz) sponge fingers

100g (3½oz) dark chocolate (70 per cent cocoa solids)

1 tablespoon cocoa powder

sugared rose petals, to decorate (optional)

FOR THE GANACHE

100g (3½oz) dark chocolate (70 per cent cocoa solids), roughly chopped

200ml (7fl oz) double cream

Put the egg yolks in a bowl with 80g (2¾oz) of the sugar and whisk with an electric whisk for 4–5 minutes until very pale and fluffy. Add the rosewater with the mascarpone and whisk until smooth. Next add the cream and whisk until it forms very soft peaks; don't overwhisk as you want the cream to be spreadable and billowy.

In another clean bowl, and with a clean electric whisk, whisk the egg whites until they form soft peaks. Add the remaining caster sugar and whisk until combined. Fold this into the egg yolk mixture.

For the ganache, put the chocolate in a heatproof bowl. Heat the cream in a saucepan. Once it is almost boiling, pour carefully over the chocolate. Let it sit for a few seconds, then stir until melted.

Find a 25cm (10 inch) bowl, 5–7.5cm (2–3 inches) deep.

In a bowl, mix the coffee and measured boiling water, then add the liqueur and mix well. Take 1 sponge finger at a time and dip it into the hot coffee mix, then place it in your chosen bowl. Continue to line the bowl with a whole layer of sponge fingers. Spread half the mascarpone cream on top and follow with all the chocolate ganache.

Repeat this to make another layer of dipped sponge fingers and mascarpone cream. Grate the chocolate over the top, sprinkle with the cocoa powder and decorate with rose petals, if you wish. Chill in the refrigerator for at least a few hours, or ideally overnight.

This can be stored in the refrigerator for 3–4 days.

This has a shortcrust, slightly sweet pastry filled with a rich and nutty brownie and a hint of cream cheese which adds to the richness. This tart is simple yet decadent and worthy of any celebration.

Brownie pecan tart

FOR THE PASTRY

200g (7oz) plain flour, plus more for dusting

pinch of fine sea salt

100g (3½oz) unsalted butter, chilled and chopped into small cubes

30g (1oz) golden caster sugar

1 egg yolk

2 tablespoons water

1 teaspoon lemon juice

FOR THE BROWNIE FILLING

100g (3½oz) dark chocolate (70 per cent cocoa solids)

100g (3½oz) unsalted butter

100g (3½oz) golden caster sugar

50g (1¾oz) light soft brown sugar

2 large eggs

50g (1¾oz) full-fat cream cheese

1 teaspoon vanilla extract

60g (2¼oz) plain flour

20g (¾oz) cocoa powder

100g (3½oz) pecan nuts, roughly chopped

TO SERVE

icing sugar

double cream

In a bowl, mix the flour and salt and add the butter. Rub the butter into the flour until you get a crumb texture, then mix in the sugar. In a separate small bowl, mix the egg, measured water and lemon juice. Add this 1 tablespoon at a time. You may not need to add it all, just enough to form a soft dough. Knead for a few seconds, then cover and rest in the refrigerator for 15 minutes.

Preheat the oven to 180°C (350°F), Gas Mark 4.

Roll out the pastry on a lightly floured surface to a 2mm- ($1/8$ inch-) thick circle and use it to line a 23cm (9 inch) tart tin, leaving any excess hanging. Prick all over the base with a fork. Line it with a large sheet of nonstick baking paper and fill with baking beans. Bake for 20 minutes. Remove the paper and beans and bake for another 15 minutes until golden and crisp. Cut off any excess pastry.

Melt the chocolate and butter in a heatproof bowl set over a saucepan of boiling water. Set aside to cool slightly. In another bowl, whisk the sugars and eggs for 5 minutes until creamy, pale and fluffy. Add the melted chocolate and whisk to combine. Add the cream cheese and vanilla and whisk again. Fold in the flour and cocoa powder, then pour into the tart tin and sprinkle with the nuts.

Bake for 30 minutes until slightly set. Set aside to cool before removing from the tin.

Dust with icing sugar and serve with cream. Any leftovers can be stored in an airtight container for 2–3 days.

Frangipane is something I have always enjoyed: the intense almond flavour and very delicate texture is simply delicious. In this recipe I have added another texture, encasing the frangipane with crispy filo pastry, while a nutty base gives it a lovely crunch.

Nutty frangipane filo tart

SERVES 8–10

150g (5½oz) unsalted butter, softened, plus 60g (2¼oz) melted, plus more for the tin

150g (5½oz) golden caster sugar

150g (5½oz) ground almonds

2 large eggs

6 sheets of filo pastry

30g (1oz) walnuts, finely chopped

30g (1oz) pistachios, finely chopped, plus a handful to finish

few drops of clear honey

Preheat the oven to 180°C (350°F), Gas Mark 4.

With an electric whisk, cream the butter and sugar in a bowl until light and fluffy (roughly 2 minutes), then add the ground almonds and eggs and mix well.

Butter a 23cm (9 inch) tart tin and place a sheet of filo inside. Brush it generously with some of the melted butter. Lay over another sheet of filo, leaving the sides overhanging the tin and brush with butter. Repeat to use all the filo, buttering each layer.

Sprinkle the chopped nuts over the filo and spoon over the frangipane. Now gently fold over the overhanging pastry to cover the filling, folding over one layer at a time. Brush it all well with the remaining butter and sprinkle some pistachios on top

Bake for 35–40 minutes.

Remove the tart from the tin and place it on a serving plate. Drizzle some honey on top and enjoy warm, on its own or with ice cream.

Best eaten the day you make it, after that the pastry starts to soften.

Hot puddings are a great thing to make and eat in the cold weather, there is something so comforting and warming about them. Whether you enjoy this with cold ice cream, add more depth with some double cream, or just enjoy it on its own, this chocolate pudding has a lovely puddle of sauce at the bottom. The addition of cinnamon and cardamom would make anyone go for seconds.

Chocolate and coconut spiced self-saucing pudding

SERVES 6–8

FOR THE PUDDING

150g (5½oz) unsalted butter, softened, plus more for the dish

150g (5½oz) golden caster sugar

3 large eggs

1 teaspoon ground cinnamon

1 teaspoon ground cardamom

1 teaspoon baking powder

100g (3½oz) self-raising flour

50g (1¾oz) cocoa powder

100g (3½oz) dark chocolate chips

FOR THE SAUCE

50g (1¾oz) light soft brown sugar

20g (¾oz) cocoa powder

4 teaspoons boiling water

400ml (14fl oz) can of good-quality, full-fat coconut milk

Preheat the oven to 180°C (350°F), Gas Mark 4. Butter a baking dish of 1.7 litre (3 pint) capacity that is at least 7.5cm (3 inches) deep.

In a bowl, using an electric whisk, beat the butter and sugar for a couple of minutes until pale and fluffy. Now add the rest of the ingredients, except for the chocolate chips, and whisk for another minute. Add the chocolate chips and fold them in. Transfer the batter to the prepared baking dish.

Make the sauce in a separate bowl, mixing the sugar, cocoa powder and measured boiling water until it forms a smooth paste. Now add the coconut milk and whisk it together. Pour this very gently and evenly over the batter and bake for 35–45 minutes.

Serve it warm with some ice cream or double cream.

This is inspired by the Spanish Basque burnt cheesecake that has become more popular over the last few years, thanks to social media. I love the rustic look of this cheesecake as well as its very creamy texture. Adding a light rose and cardamom flavour gives Indian-inspired aroma and fragrance to this stunning cheesecake.

Rose and cardamom cheesecake

SERVES 8–10

unsalted butter, for the tin

600g (1lb 5oz) full-fat cream cheese

150g (5½oz) golden caster sugar

4 large eggs

1 teaspoon rosewater

1 teaspoon ground cardamom

½ teaspoon fine sea salt

200ml (7fl oz) double cream

40g (1½oz) plain flour, sifted

Preheat the oven to 220°C (425°F), Gas Mark 7. Butter a 20cm (8 inch) round springform cake tin and cut out a round piece of nonstick baking paper about 5cm (2 inches) bigger than the diameter of the tin and its sides. Line the tin with this, leaving the excess paper above the tin.

Put the cream cheese and sugar in a large bowl and mix together until smooth. Now add 1 egg at a time and whisk with an electric whisk until combined. Add the rosewater, cardamom, salt and cream and mix well.

Continuing to whisk, slowly add the flour, 1 tablespoon at a time, until everything is well combined. Whisk for 1 minute more, then pour into the prepared tin.

Place the tin on a baking tray and bake the cheesecake for 40–45 minutes until the top is browned and the middle is still wobbly. Leave it in the tin to cool completely. The cheesecake will sink and set once it has cooled, and that is how it is supposed to be. You can enjoy this at room temperature, or leave it to chill in the refrigerator overnight.

Store it in the refrigerator for 2–3 days.

A blend of cake and bread topped with cream… what's not to like? This yeasted cake with a seam of citrusy orange running through it is showered in orange liqueur syrup and topped with cinnamon cream. I was introduced to it when we were asked to bake a yeasted cake from Europe on the *Great British Bake Off*. I love the lightness of the sponge, oozing syrup in every bite, as well as the creaminess and warmth of the cinnamon topping. You must try it.

Orange and cinnamon savarin

SERVES 10–12

FOR THE CAKE

150g (5½oz) unsalted butter, melted, plus more for the tin

350g (12oz) plain flour, plus more for the tin

4 large eggs

40g (1½oz) caster sugar

finely grated zest of 2 oranges, plus extra to decorate

1 teaspoon vanilla extract

½ teaspoon fine sea salt

7g (¼oz) fast-action dried yeast

250ml (9fl oz) lukewarm whole milk

a little neutral-tasting oil (optional)

Butter a 25cm (10 inch) savarin tin and dust with flour.

Beat the eggs and sugar in a bowl with an electric whisk until creamy and pale. Add the orange zest, vanilla, salt and melted butter and whisk well. In another bowl, beat together the flour, yeast and lukewarm milk. Add the egg mix to the flour mix and combine it all together with a wooden spoon until you have a smooth pouring batter.

Cover and let it prove for 15–20 minutes until it bubbles up slightly.

Using a wooden spoon, beat the air out, then transfer the batter to the prepared tin, cover and let it rest for 1 hour or until it doubles in size. If using clingfilm to cover, make sure you oil the clingfilm so that it doesn't stick to the batter when it rises.

Preheat the oven to 200°C (400°F), Gas Mark 6. Bake the savarin for 30–40 minutes or until done. Leave it in the tin for 5 minutes, then turn it out and place on a shallow serving plate with a little lip, so it can hold the syrup.

FOR THE SYRUP

6 tablespoons fresh orange juice

4 tablespoons orange liqueur

250ml (9fl oz) water

150g (5½oz) caster sugar

FOR THE FILLING

500ml (18fl oz) double cream

100g (3½oz) caster sugar

1 teaspoon ground cinnamon

Meanwhile, prepare the syrup by heating the orange juice, liqueur, measured water and sugar in a saucepan until the sugar has dissolved. Simmer for 5 minutes.

Spoon the syrup evenly and gradually over the still warm savarin, letting the crumb absorb the syrup. Leave to cool.

Whip the cream, sugar and cinnamon until it forms soft peaks. Once the savarin has cooled, pipe or spread the cream on top, sprinkle over the extra orange zest and serve.

This can be stored in an airtight container in the refrigerator for 3–4 days.

A stunning centrepiece for any celebration, based on a Hungarian recipe – dobos torte – with six layers of sponge brushed with amaretto syrup. It is all sandwiched by the most delicious chocolate buttercream. I finish this cake with caramel curls formed around grapes, a technique I came up with in the tent on the *Great British Bake Off* which I decided to dust off again.

Almond and caramel torte with chocolate buttercream

SERVES 8–10

FOR THE CAKE

6 large eggs

250g (9oz) caster sugar

200g (7oz) self-raising flour

FOR THE SYRUP

100ml (3½fl oz) amaretto

75g (2¾oz) caster sugar

5 tablespoons water

FOR THE BUTTERCREAM

300g (10½oz) dark chocolate (70 per cent cocoa solids), melted

4 large eggs

200g (7oz) caster sugar

250g (9oz) unsalted butter, softened

1 teaspoon vanilla extract

FOR THE CARAMEL CURLS (OPTIONAL)

bunch of grapes

a little neutral-tasting oil

200g (7oz) caster sugar

100ml (3½fl oz) water

Preheat the oven to 180°C (350°F), Gas Mark 4. Draw 6 x 20cm (8 inch) circles on pieces of nonstick baking paper and place them spaced apart on baking trays, turning the sheets over so the pencil marks are on the bottom but still visible. Depending on the size of your baking trays, you may need 3 or 4.

In a large bowl, beat the eggs and sugar with an electric whisk for a good 8–10 minutes until pale and creamy and the batter leaves a trail when the whisk is lifted. Now sift the self-raising flour on to the egg mix and very carefully fold it all in without losing much air. Spread around 120g (4½oz) of the cake batter on each drawn circle and bake for 8 minutes, or until done. Depending on the size of your oven, you may need to cook the sponges in batches. Set aside to cool.

Meanwhile, prepare the syrup by putting the amaretto, sugar and measured water in a saucepan and bring to the boil, stirring until the sugar has dissolved. Set aside to cool slightly. Brush this syrup on all the cake layers.

While the cakes are cooling, start preparing the buttercream. Break the chocolate into a heatproof bowl and set it over a saucepan of simmering water until melted (make sure the bowl does not touch the water). Set aside to cool.

continued overleaf

Combine the eggs and sugar in another heatproof bowl, place it over the same pan of simmering water and beat the eggs with an electric whisk for 10 minutes until thickened and creamy. Remove from the pan and continue to whisk for another 8–10 minutes until it cools down. The mixture should resemble meringue but without the peaks.

Now add the cooled melted chocolate and whisk until combined. Put the butter and vanilla in a bowl and beat it with a wooden spoon until smooth. Now add a little bit of the butter mix to the chocolate mix and whisk it in, continuing until all the butter has been added.

To assemble the cake, place a layer of sponge on a serving dish and spread on some of the buttercream, then repeat with another cake and another layer of buttercream until all the layers are on. Cover the cake with the leftover buttercream and smooth it out. Leave it in the refrigerator to set slightly.

If you want to decorate the cake, remove a bunch of grapes from the stem and lightly oil them. Insert a toothpick into each grape and place on an oiled baking tray. Make a caramel by putting the sugar and water in a saucepan and cooking until golden brown. Pick up a grape by the toothpick and carefully dip half of it into the caramel. Place the grape on its head and set aside for the caramel to set. Repeat with the remaining grapes. Carefully peel the caramel curls from the grapes, place on the cake and serve.

You can store the torte, covered, in the refrigerator for 3–4 days, but expect the caramel curls to melt during this time. Bring to room temperature before serving.

This is inspired by the amazing povitica, an Eastern European bread which I came across for the first time many years ago in the *Bake Off* tent. This is such a lovely soft stretchy dough, filled with nutty chocolate spread and made richer with the dates and a slight hint of spice. A crowd-pleaser: from kids to grown-ups, this is loved by all.

Walnut and date swirl bread

SERVES 8–10

FOR THE DOUGH

160ml (5½fl oz) lukewarm whole milk, plus 1 tablespoon if needed

60g (2¼oz) unsalted butter, melted, plus more for the tin

1 large egg, lightly beaten

300g (10½oz) strong white bread flour, plus more for dusting

5g (⅛oz) fine sea salt

10g (¼oz) fast-action dried yeast

1 egg white, lightly beaten, for glazing

FOR THE FILLING

100g (3½oz) medjool dates

2 tablespoons whole milk

200g (7oz) walnuts, blitzed to a powder

1 teaspoon ground cardamom

1 teaspoon ground cinnamon

80g (2¾oz) light soft brown sugar

2 tablespoons cocoa powder

100g (3½oz) dark chocolate (70 per cent cocoa solids), melted (see page 38)

100g (3½oz) unsalted butter, melted

Start with the dough, which you can make by hand or in a food mixer fitted with the dough hook. Put the milk, butter and whole egg (reserve the egg white for glazing later) in a bowl and mix together. In a separate big bowl, mix the flour, salt and yeast, then slowly pour in the liquid, bringing it together into a soft dough. Knead for 8–10 minutes until stretchy and smooth. Cover and prove for 1–2 hours until doubled in size.

Once the dough is ready, prepare the filling. Blitz the dates with the milk and transfer to a bowl with the rest of the ingredients. Mix well. Butter a 900g (2lb) loaf tin.

Dust a large work surface with flour. Roll out the dough into a rectangle, roughly 50 x 25cm (20 x 10 inches). Dust your hands with flour and gently stretch the dough from underneath with the help of your hands. Don't rush this: stretch slowly and evenly from all sides, stretching the dough outwards from the centre until you have a translucent sheet, roughly 100 x 50cm (40 x 20 inches). Very gently spread the filling all over the dough. If the filling is too thick, add 1 tablespoon of warm milk to loosen it.

continued overleaf

Starting from a long side of the dough, roll it up tightly like a Swiss roll. Lift the roll from one end and carefully coil it into the buttered loaf tin, starting from one end and shaping it into a "U" and then another "U", until the whole roll is used up. Cover and let it prove for 1 hour, or until risen a little.

Preheat the oven to 180°C (350°F), Gas Mark 4.

Brush the loaf with the egg white. Bake the loaf for 15 minutes. Reduce the oven temperature to 150°C (300°F), Gas Mark 2 and bake for another 45–50 minutes until golden brown. If the top begins to brown too quickly, cover it with foil.

Once baked, let it sit for 10 minutes in the loaf tin, then turn it out on to a wire rack to cool completely.

Enjoy it fresh, or store it in an airtight container for 2–3 days.

For this cake I took inspiration from the Swedish "princess" cake. The light sponge is sandwiched with an airy custard cream and a thin layer of raspberry jam gives it that fresh kick. I absolutely love this and would happily have a slice or two (sometimes three) in one sitting. It's subtle flavours make it so dreamy.

Almond and cardamom custard cake

SERVES 8–10

FOR THE CAKE

50g (1¾oz) unsalted butter, melted, plus more for the tin

4 large eggs

150g (5½oz) golden caster sugar

70g (2½oz) cornflour

50g (1¾oz) plain flour

20g (¾oz) ground almonds

1 teaspoon baking powder

½ teaspoon almond extract

FOR THE CUSTARD

600ml (20fl oz) whole milk

1 teaspoon ground cardamom

6 egg yolks

100g (3½oz) caster sugar

40g (1½oz) cornflour

50g (1¾oz) unsalted butter

TO ASSEMBLE

600ml (20fl oz) double cream

2 tablespoons caster sugar

6 tablespoons Raspberry cardamom jam (see page 192)

Preheat the oven to 180°C (350°F), Gas Mark 4. Butter a 20cm (8 in) round deep cake tin and line it with nonstick baking paper.

Put the eggs and sugar in the bowl of a food mixer fitted with the whisk attachment and whisk for 6–8 minutes until pale and fluffy: when you lift the whisk, the batter should leave a trail (this is known as the "ribbon stage").

Sift the cornflour, plain flour, ground almonds and baking powder into another bowl. Place the sieve over the egg mixture and sift the flour mix again on top of the eggs. Fold it all gently together without losing much air. Next drizzle the butter and almond extract on top of the batter and fold in.

Transfer to the prepared cake tin. Bake for 20–25 minutes until baked and the cake leaves the sides of the tin. Set aside to cool completely.

In the meantime, prepare the custard. In a saucepan, heat the milk and cardamom until it just begins to boil. In a bowl, whisk the egg yolks with the sugar and cornflour until pale and creamy. Slowly add the hot milk to the eggs and whisk continuously.

Return this mixture to the pan and cook over a low heat for 5–6 minutes until the custard has thickened. Pass it through a sieve into a bowl, add the butter and mix until melted. Put a layer of clingfilm directly on the surface of the custard, to stop it from forming a skin. Chill in the refrigerator.

When ready to assemble, whisk the cream and sugar with an electric whisk until it forms soft peaks. Now add the chilled custard and fold it all in.

With a sharp knife, cut the cake horizontally into 3 layers. Line the cake tin in which you baked the sponge with clingfilm.

Take the first layer of cake, put half the jam on top and spread it over evenly. Place this cake layer into the lined cake tin, jam-side up. Spread one-third of the custard cream on top.

Take the second layer of cake, spread with the remaining jam and place over the cake in the tin. Spread one-third more of the custard cream on top.

Top with the final cake layer and spread over the remaining custard cream.

Cover with clingfilm and let it chill in the refrigerator for good few hours, ideally overnight.

Remove from the tin, peel off the clingfilm and serve.

This cake can be stored in an airtight container in the refrigerator for 3–4 days.

Something savoury

Rainbow chard masala pasty

Chana dal-stuffed yogurt bread

Roasted cauliflower katchapuri

Masala chicken pepper pie

Paneer and Cheddar scones

Spiced lentil filo rolls

Curried chickpea cauliflower pie
with fenugreek pastry

Turmeric brioche rolls

Chilli naan pizza

Coriander, sweetcorn and feta loaf

Chutney cheese twists

Giant onion cheese spiral

Spicy coriander chicken bake

Mattar paneer pie

A crispy pasty stuffed with spicy filling: that's right, there is definitely something to smile about! The chard and potato filling is ready in minutes and so is the pastry, so all that's left to do is to put the two together and bake! Enjoy these warm, with some salad or a chutney, or pack for your lunch or a picnic and – dare I say – eat with ketchup.

Rainbow chard masala pasty

MAKES 4

FOR THE PASTRY

400g (14oz) plain flour, plus more for dusting

170g (5¾oz) unsalted butter, chilled and chopped into small cubes

1 teaspoon fine sea salt

1 egg yolk

140ml (4½fl oz) water

1 egg, lightly beaten

FOR THE FILLING

2 tablespoons sunflower oil

1 teaspoon cumin seeds

1 large onion, finely chopped

2 garlic cloves, finely chopped

1 bird's eye green chilli, finely chopped

2 medium potatoes, peeled and cut into small cubes

1 teaspoon ground turmeric

1 teaspoon chilli powder

2 teaspoons garam masala

1 teaspoon salt

300g (10½oz) rainbow chard, finely chopped

Put the flour and butter in a bowl and rub with your fingers until you get a crumb texture. Add the salt and egg yolk and combine it well. Slowly add the water, a little at a time, until it comes together in a dough. Knead for a few seconds, then wrap it in clingfilm and let it rest in the refrigerator for 20–30 minutes.

To prepare the filling, heat the oil in a saucepan and add the cumin seeds. Once they start sizzling, add the onion. Cook over a medium-low heat for 5 minutes until lightly golden. Add the garlic and chilli and cook for a few seconds. Then add the potatoes, spices and salt with 2 tablespoons of water, cover and cook for 10 minutes over a low heat. Once the potatoes are soft and cooked, add the chard. Mix well, then cover and cook for another 10 minutes. Transfer the mixture to a bowl and let it cool.

Preheat the oven to 200°C (400°F), Gas Mark 6. Line 2 baking trays with nonstick baking paper.

Divide the pastry into 4 equal portions. Roll each out on a floured work surface into a circle, using a dinner plate 20–22.5cm (8–9 inches) in diameter as a template. Place one-quarter of the filling on the centre of each circle. Brush the egg around the edges. Fold the pastry over the filling and pinch together to seal.

Brush the remaining egg all over the pasties. Bake for 35–40 minutes until golden and crispy. Enjoy them piping hot, or at room temperature.

Dal is great with any bread: whether it is naan, chapati, paratha or even a piece of toast, bread is the perfect edible scoop. This dough is inspired by bhatura – a deep-fried bread from north India – and the filling is luscious chana dal, which I cook often to eat with rotis. Here, I have combined them into one meal of pillowy-soft dough with a delicious lentil-feta filling.

Chana dal-stuffed yogurt bread

MAKES 4

FOR THE FILLING

200g (7oz) chana dal

700ml (1¼ pints) water

½ teaspoon salt

½ teaspoon ground turmeric

10g (¼oz) fresh coriander, finely chopped

1 bird's eye green chilli, finely chopped

200g (7oz) feta cheese, finely crumbled

FOR THE DOUGH

200g (7oz) natural yogurt

1 teaspoon sunflower oil

1 teaspoon lemon juice

300g (10½oz) plain flour, plus more for dusting

½ teaspoon caster sugar

½ teaspoon fine sea salt

1 teaspoon bicarbonate of soda

4 teaspoons salted butter

Put the dal, measured water, salt and turmeric in a saucepan and bring to the boil over a medium-high heat. Cover and cook for 40–45 minutes until soft and cooked through: the water should all have been absorbed and the mixture should be soft. If there is any liquid left, cook, uncovered, over a high heat until it has evaporated.

Transfer to a bowl to cool. Once cool, add the coriander, chilli and feta and mix well.

In another bowl, combine the yogurt, oil and lemon juice and mix well. Put the flour, sugar, salt and bicarbonate of soda in a separate large bowl and slowly add the yogurt mixture. Bring it together into a soft dough and knead it for a few seconds. Divide into 4 portions.

Cover each portion in flour. Roll the first portion out into a 20–23cm (8–9 inch) circle. Place one-quarter of the lentils in the middle of the circle and flatten it out, leaving a 5cm (2 inch) border around the edges. Pick up one edge of the circle and fold it into the middle. Keep folding in the edges until the filling is covered. Lightly flatten the filled bread with a rolling pin, so that all the edges are sealed. Repeat to fill and seal all 4 breads.

Heat a flat pan or a skillet and cook each bread for roughly 2 minutes on each side until golden. Brush each with 1 teaspoon of butter and serve, or keep warm in some foil or a tea towel while you cook the rest. Serve them warm and fresh.

Katchapuri is something I came across last year when my friend Katie Quinn wrote about it in her book *Cheese, wine, and bread*; that inspired me to bake it for the first time… and I loved it. I have made it here with roasted cauliflower, something I enjoy a lot. Cheese-filled dough topped with roasted cauliflower: everything about this is delicious.

Roasted cauliflower katchapuri

SERVES 4

FOR THE DOUGH

250g (9oz) plain flour, plus more for dusting

½ teaspoon fine sea salt

½ teaspoon baking powder

1 teaspoon ground turmeric

1 teaspoon cumin seeds

200g (7oz) natural yogurt

1 teaspoon salted butter, melted

1 tablespoon rapeseed oil

1 egg, lightly beaten

FOR THE CAULIFLOWER

1 tablespoon rapeseed oil

1 tablespoon tomato purée

¼ teaspoon fine sea salt

½ teaspoon chilli powder

200g (7oz) cauliflower, cut into small florets, smaller leaves reserved

FOR THE FILLING

100g (3½oz) mozzarella cheese, crumbled

100g (3½oz) feta cheese, crumbled

1 large egg, lightly beaten

Start with the dough. Put the flour, salt, baking powder, turmeric and cumin in a bowl. Add the yogurt, butter and oil and mix well. Bring it together into a dough, knead it for a few seconds, then cover and let it rest for 1 hour.

Meanwhile, preheat the oven to 180°C (350°F), Gas Mark 4 and prepare the cauliflower and cheese filling.

Combine the cauliflower ingredients in a small bowl and mix well. Tip on to a baking tray and roast for 10 minutes. Set aside to cool.

Make the cheese filling by combining the cheeses and the egg in another small, clean bowl.

When you're ready to bake the katchapuri, preheat the oven to 200°C (400°F), Gas Mark 6 and lightly flour a baking tray.

Place the dough on a lightly floured work surface and knead for 2 minutes until smooth. Roll it into a 30cm (12 inch) circle. Transfer this to the prepared tray. Arrange the cheese filling around the top and bottom curves of the circle, 2.5cm (1 in) from the edge. Fold the edges of the dough over the cheese and press to seal. Pinch the 2 sides, shaping it into a boat. Now fill the centre with the cauliflower.

Brush the dough with the beaten egg and bake for 20–25 minutes until golden.

Cut into pieces and serve warm, on the same day it is baked.

Chicken curry is one of my top comfort foods, I love it when the chicken and spices marry together with lots of onions and garlic, as they do here. This recipe uses a delicious chicken curry as the pie filling, topped with flaky filo pastry.

SERVES 4

2 tablespoons coriander seeds

2 tablespoons sunflower oil

1 teaspoon fenugreek seeds

2 medium-sized onions, finely sliced

1 bird's eye green chilli, finely chopped

4 garlic cloves, finely chopped

2.5cm (1 inch) piece of fresh root ginger, finely chopped

400g (14oz) can of chopped tomatoes

1 teaspoon salt

1 teaspoon garam masala

½ teaspoon chilli powder

8 skinless boneless chicken thighs, cut into bite-sized pieces

1 green pepper, roughly chopped

4 tablespoons double cream

20g (¾oz) fresh coriander leaves, roughly chopped

270g (9½oz) pack of ready-rolled filo pastry

25g (1oz) salted butter, melted

Masala chicken pepper pie

Heat a wide, shallow pan (with a lid) and add the coriander seeds. Dry-toast them for a minute or so until they are fragrant and have changed colour slightly. Remove them to a mortar and pestle and crush to a powder.

Heat the oil in the same pan and add the fenugreek seeds. Once they start to pop, add the onions and chilli and cook over a medium-low heat for 10 minutes until golden. Add the garlic and ginger and cook for another minute. Next add the tomatoes. Cover and cook for 5 minutes until everything comes together.

Stir in the salt and ground spices and the crushed coriander seeds. Follow with the chicken and pepper, cover and cook for 10 minutes until the chicken is done. Remove from the heat, stir in the cream and coriander leaves and transfer to a 23cm (9 inch) pie dish. Let it cool slightly.

Preheat the oven to 200°C (400°F), Gas Mark 6.

Unroll the pastry, brush each sheet with the melted butter and then tear and scrunch the sheets on top of the chicken filling.

Bake for 25–30 minutes until golden. Let it sit for 5 minutes before serving.

What is better than warm cheese scones? I'll tell you what: these spicy, aromatic paneer cheese scones. Cut them open and spread in some butter, then a layer of Onion chutney or Very spicy apple chutney (see page 198), sit back and enjoy!

Paneer and Cheddar scones

MAKES 8–10

230g (8¼oz) self-raising flour, plus more for dusting

¼ teaspoon fine sea salt

¼ teaspoon freshly ground black pepper

1 teaspoon baking powder

60g (2¼oz) unsalted butter, chilled and chopped into small cubes

100g (3½oz) Cheddar cheese, grated

40g (1½oz) paneer cheese, grated

20g (¾oz) fresh coriander leaves, finely chopped

1 bird's eye green chilli, finely chopped

180ml (6fl oz) buttermilk

1 egg, lightly beaten

Preheat the oven to 200°C (400°F, Gas Mark 6. Line 2 baking trays with nonstick baking paper.

In a bowl, combine the flour, salt, pepper and baking powder. Add the butter and rub it into the flour with your hands until you get a crumb texture. Next, stir in the Cheddar, paneer, coriander and chilli and mix well.

Slowly add the buttermilk and bring the mixture together into a dough. Don't knead it too much, as it will make the scones hard.

On a lightly floured work surface, roll the dough out gently until 2cm (¾ inch) thick. Take a 6cm (2½ inch) round cutter and cut out scones. Bring together the leftover dough and roll it out again, then cut out more scones. Place them all on the prepared trays and brush the tops with egg. Bake for 20 minutes until golden.

Serve warm with butter and chutney. Enjoy them within a couple of days.

I always have a variety of lentils in my cupboard, as they are something I cook with all the time. They form my Monday evening meal most weeks, as they are delicious, creamy and comforting. So I decided to make a lovely snack with them by wrapping lightly spiced brown lentils in crispy filo pastry. You can enjoy these lovely little filo rolls with some Coriander chutney (see page 195).

Spiced lentil filo rolls

MAKES 12

2 tablespoons sunflower oil

1 teaspoon cumin seeds

1 medium onion, finely chopped

1 bird's eye green chilli, finely chopped

1 teaspoon salt

½ teaspoon ground turmeric

1 teaspoon ground coriander

150g (5½oz) whole masoor dal

400ml (14fl oz) water, or as needed

12 sheets of filo pastry

100g (3½oz) salted butter, melted

Heat the oil in a saucepan and add the cumin seeds. Once they start to sizzle, add the onion and chilli and cook over a medium heat for 6–8 minutes until golden.

Add the salt, spices, then the lentils and mix well. Now pour in the measured water and bring to the boil. Cover and cook over a low heat for 40 minutes or until the lentils are cooked and soft. Check them halfway through in case the pan has dried out; if it has, add some more water. The cooked mixture should be soft and the liquid should have been absorbed. Set aside to cool completely.

Preheat the oven to 200°C (400°F), Gas Mark 6. Line 2 baking sheets with nonstick baking paper.

Unroll a sheet of filo and place it on a work surface with a short side facing you. Cover the rest of the sheets with a damp tea towel, otherwise they will dry out.

Put 1–2 tablespoons of the cold lentil mixture in the bottom centre of the pastry and brush the rest of the pastry with melted butter. Fold the sides in, then roll it away from you, sealing the lentils and making a cigar shape. Brush with butter and place on one of the prepared trays. Repeat to fill and roll the remaining filo sheets.

Bake for 25–30 minutes until golden and crispy. Let them rest for 5 minutes, then serve them warm or at room temperature. These are best enjoyed on the day they are baked.

I am a big fan of pies – they are a complete meal – and since I don't eat any meat other than chicken, I love playing around with vegetarian versions. This spicy, vibrant filling is the perfect partner for the crumbly pastry. Serve this with some Jaggery and tamarind raita (see page 200) and you have a plate of delicious comfort food.

Curried chickpea cauliflower pie with fenugreek pastry

SERVES 4

FOR THE FILLING

2 tablespoons sunflower oil

1 teaspoon cumin seeds

1 medium-sized onion, finely chopped

1 bird's eye green chilli, finely chopped

2 garlic cloves, finely chopped

2 medium-sized tomatoes, roughly chopped

1 teaspoon fine sea salt

1 teaspoon chilli powder

1 teaspoon ground turmeric

1 teaspoon garam masala

¼ cauliflower, cut into 5cm (2 inch) florets

1 medium-sized potato, peeled and cut into 2.5cm (1 inch) cubes

400g (14oz) can of chickpeas, drained and rinsed

100ml (3½fl oz) water

FOR THE PASTRY

300g (10½oz) plain flour, plus more for dusting

½ teaspoon fine sea salt

½ teaspoon chilli powder

150g (5½oz) unsalted butter, chilled and chopped into cubes

1 tablespoon dried fenugreek leaves

5–6 tablespoons water

1 egg, lightly beaten

Start with the filling. Heat the oil in a saucepan and add the cumin seeds. Once they start to sizzle, add the onion and chilli and cook for 10 minutes until golden. Next, add the garlic and cook for another minute before adding the tomatoes. Cover and cook over a low heat for 5 minutes until they start to soften.

Next, add the salt and all the spices, then after a few seconds add the cauliflower, potato, chickpeas and measured water and mix well. Cover and cook for 10 minutes until the vegetables begin to soften (they don't need to cook completely). Transfer the chickpea mixture to a pie tin about 23cm (9 inches) in diameter.

Meanwhile, prepare the pastry by mixing the flour, salt and chilli. Next, add the butter and rub it well into the flour until you have a crumb texture. Now add the fenugreek leaves and mix well. Slowly add the measured water and mix until you get nice soft dough (you may not need all the water). Knead for a few seconds, then cover and refrigerate for 30 minutes.

Preheat the oven to 200°C (400°F), Gas Mark 6.

continued overleaf

On a lightly floured work surface, roll the pastry out to 3mm (1/8 inch) thick. Cut away a long thin strip that is 1cm (1/2 inch) thick. Dampen the rim of the pie dish with water, then press down the dough strip along the rim. Dampen the dough strip too. Cover the pie with the remaining dough sheet and press down on the rim, sealing the pie. Trim off the excess and crimp the sides in any pattern you like. Make a little slit in the middle of the dough to let out some steam. If you want to decorate the pie, make a floral pattern with the leftover dough and stick it on by brushing with water.

Brush the pie generously all over with the beaten egg and bake for 40 minutes until golden. Let it sit for 5 minutes before serving hot.

A soft brioche roll to make that perfect sandwich, or just to enjoy with good salted butter. These are lightly flavoured with the turmeric that also adds the lovely colour to the rolls.

Turmeric brioche rolls

MAKES 8

320g (11½oz) strong white bread flour, plus extra for dusting

1 teaspoon fine sea salt

1½ teaspoons fast-action dried yeast

1 tablespoon caster sugar

50g (1¾oz) unsalted butter, softened, plus more for the bowl

1 large egg, lightly beaten, plus 1 more for the egg wash

120ml (4fl oz) lukewarm water

2 tablespoons whole milk

1 teaspoon ground turmeric

1 teaspoon nigella seeds

Put the flour, salt, yeast and sugar in a bowl and mix well. Add the butter and rub it into the flour until you get a crumb texture.

In another bowl, mix the egg, measured lukewarm water, milk and turmeric. Add this to the flour and bring it together into a dough. Put the mixture in the bowl of a food mixer fitted with a dough hook – or on a lightly floured work surface – and knead for 8–10 minutes until smooth and stretchy.

Lightly butter a bowl, put the dough into it, cover and let it prove for 2 hours, or until doubled in size.

Divide the dough into 8 portions (roughly 70g/2½oz each) and shape each into a small (roughly 7.5cm/3 inch) roll. Place on a lightly floured baking tray, cover and let prove for 1 hour, or until doubled in size. Brush with egg and sprinkle the nigella seeds on top.

Preheat the oven to 200°C (400°F), Gas Mark 6. Bake the rolls for 18–20 minutes until golden and cooked. Let them cool before serving.

Wrap them up in muslin, foil or a clean tea towel and they will store well for 2–3 days.

This recipe is in no way disrespecting either naan or pizza, as I love them both dearly, but I've started to combine them. I love the texture of naan dough and the cheesy topping of pizza, so it only makes sense for me to present this naan-pizza combination. Here I use my favourite coriander chutney with the cheese, but feel free to add your chosen toppings. You can cook the breads a few hours in advance and grill with the cheese topping just before serving.

Chilli naan pizza

MAKES 4

FOR THE DOUGH

300g (10½oz) strong white bread flour, plus more for dusting

1 teaspoon caster sugar

1 teaspoon fine sea salt

7g (¼oz) fast-action dried yeast

2 tablespoons natural yogurt

150ml (5fl oz) whole milk

2 teaspoons salted butter

FOR THE TOPPING

100g (3½oz) Cheddar cheese, grated

100g (3½oz) mozzarella cheese, grated

1 red onion, finely chopped

1 teaspoon chilli flakes

1 bird's eye green chilli, finely chopped

Coriander chutney (see page 195)

Put the flour, sugar, salt and yeast in a bowl and mix well. Next, add the yogurt, slowly pour in the milk and bring it together into a soft dough. Knead for 2 minutes, then cover and let it rest for 1 hour.

Preheat the grill to medium. Divide the dough into 4 portions. Roll each piece out on a lightly floured surface into a circle about 20cm (8 inches) in diameter. Place on a lightly floured baking tray and put it under the grill for 1 minute until golden, then turn it over and cook for another minute. Spread ½ teaspoon butter on top. Repeat to cook all the naans.

In a bowl, mix the cheeses with the onion, chilli flakes and chilli and mix well. Now return 1 cooked naan to the baking tray. Spread some coriander chutney on top, sprinkle over one-quarter of the cheese mix and put it back under the grill for 1–2 minutes or until the cheese has melted and got some colour. Cut into pieces and serve immediately. Repeat to cook all the chilli naan pizzas. Serve immediately.

Enjoying a corn on the cob in the monsoon in Mumbai is one of those memories that always brings a smile to my face. We are lucky to have lovely canned sweetcorn available throughout the year and I put it to good use here, baking it with coriander, chilli and two cheeses. Pair it with some Coriander chutney (see page 195), or just with good butter. Great for packed lunches, picnics or just as a snack.

Coriander, sweetcorn and feta loaf

SERVES 6–8

100ml (3½fl oz) sunflower oil, plus more for the tin

200g (7oz) self-raising flour

¾ teaspoon fine sea salt

½ teaspoon baking powder

½ teaspoon bicarbonate of soda

1 bird's eye green chilli, finely chopped

20g (¾oz) fresh coriander leaves, roughly chopped

2 large eggs

30g (1oz) Cheddar cheese, grated

30g (1oz) feta cheese, crumbled into small pieces

140g (5oz) canned sweetcorn, drained

Preheat the oven to 180°C (350°F), Gas Mark 4. Oil a 900g (2lb) loaf tin and then line it with nonstick baking paper.

In a bowl, mix all the dry ingredients, chilli and coriander together. In another bowl, mix the oil, eggs and both cheeses.

Now add the egg mixture to the flour bowl with the sweetcorn and mix it all well. Pour the batter into the prepared tin and bake for 45–50 minutes until a skewer inserted comes out clean. Let the loaf sit in the tin for 5–10 minutes before turning it out. Serve it warm or at room temperature.

This can be stored in an airtight container for 2–3 days.

One of the things I tend to have in the refrigerator is ready-made puff pastry. You can make so many things with it, from parcels or tarts to little snacks like these. And I always have some form of chutney in the refrigerator too. So, I have paired my roast aubergine chutney with puff pastry to make these easy, quick snacks, but you can use any other chutney of your choice. Chutney pairs so well with the spring onions and Cheddar cheese, all encased in crispy flaky pastry, that these little twists will be very moreish whatever you choose.

Chutney cheese twists

MAKES 12–14

320g (11¼oz) pack of ready-rolled puff pastry

plain flour, for dusting

6 tablespoons Roasted aubergine chutney (see page 194)

4 spring onions, finely chopped

50g (1¾oz) Cheddar cheese, grated

1 egg, lightly beaten

Preheat the oven to 200°C (400°F), Gas Mark 6. Line 2 baking sheets with nonstick baking paper.

Unroll the pastry on a lightly floured surface, with a longer side facing you.

In a bowl, mix the chutney, spring onions and cheese. Spread this mixture on the bottom half of the pastry. Fold the top half of the pastry down over the filling and press gently to seal. Brush the pastry with the egg all over.

Cut the filled pastry rectangle vertically into 2cm (¾ inch) strips. Pick up one strip, twist it, then place on the prepared trays. Repeat with the remaining strips. Bake for 20–25 minutes until golden and crispy.

These are best enjoyed warm straight out of the oven as they do not store well.

A giant roll of soft dough filled with lovely onion chutney and crumbly feta cheese, all wrapped up into a giant spiral. This is a great bread for sharing, just bring it to the table, cut into pieces and enjoy with family and friends, or wrap it up and take to a picnic. The pastry used here is similar to filo and therefore requires a bit of attention and patience, but the finished product is totally worth it.

Giant onion cheese spiral

SERVES 8

FOR THE DOUGH

170ml (6fl oz) lukewarm water

1 large egg, lightly beaten, plus 1 more, to glaze

350g (12oz) plain flour, plus more for dusting

FOR THE FILLING

1 portion Onion chutney (see page 198)

200g (7oz) feta cheese, finely crumbled

Start with the dough. Put the measured water and 1 egg in a bowl and combine well. Tip in the flour and mix it well into a sticky, thick dough. Cover and let it rest in the refrigerator for 1 hour.

Preheat the oven to 200°C (400°F), Gas Mark 6. Line a baking sheet with nonstick baking paper.

Generously flour a large work surface (the kitchen table is good here) and knead the dough until it is no longer sticky. Divide this into 2 portions. Roll out each portion into a big circle, roughly 30cm (12 inches) in diameter. Now flour your hands well and stretch the dough from underneath, slowly and gently, until you get a translucent circular sheet of pastry, 87.5–75cm (30–35 inches) in diameter. Make sure to keep the surface well floured the whole time.

Spread a thin layer of onion chutney very gently on this circle and sprinkle half the crumbled feta on top. Now roll and stretch the second portion of dough in the same way as the first. Place it on top of the onion and feta. Spread another thin layer of onion chutney on top and sprinkle with the remaining feta.

Start rolling from one side of the circle until you have a long roll of cheese-filled pastry. Spiral the roll on to the prepared baking sheet, starting at the centre and working your way towards the edge. Brush it generously with egg and bake for 45–50 minutes until golden. Let it cool slightly before serving.

Best enjoyed fresh.

The first time I had a chicken bake it was from a high-street bakery chain, the place where I went to get my lunch every day when I worked in retail. Now my son loves them too, so I decided to transform a plain chicken bake into this spicy coriander version: it is absolutely delicious.

Spicy coriander chicken bake

MAKES 4

2 tablespoons sunflower oil

1 bird's eye green chilli, finely chopped

2 chicken breasts, cut into 1cm (½ inch) pieces

½ teaspoon chilli powder

½ teaspoon freshly ground black pepper

pinch of salt

100ml (3½fl oz) chicken stock

3 tablespoons double cream

10g (¼oz) fresh coriander leaves, finely chopped

2 tablespoons cornflour

plain flour, for dusting

320g (11½oz) packet of ready-rolled puff pastry

1 egg, lightly beaten

Heat the oil in a saucepan and add the chilli, followed by the chicken. Cook over a medium heat for 2 minutes. Add the chilli powder, pepper and salt and mix well. Pour in the stock, cover and cook over a low heat for 2–3 minutes until the chicken is cooked.

Mix in the cream and coriander leaves. Mix the cornflour in a small bowl with 2 tablespoons of cold water to form a paste. Add this to the pan and stir until the mix has thickened. Set aside to cool completely.

Preheat the oven to 200°C (400°F), Gas Mark 6. Line 2 baking sheets with nonstick baking paper.

Unroll the pastry on a lightly floured work surface and cut it into 4 portions. Put one-quarter of the chicken mixture on one half of each portion and brush the pastry edges with egg. Fold the pastry over to cover the filling and seal the parcels by pressing a fork on the border to seal them well.

Place the parcels on the prepared baking sheets and brush all over with the remaining egg. Bake for 20–25 minutes until crispy and golden and serve warm.

This peas and paneer filling is my take on my mum's proper Punjabi mattar paneer (pea and paneer) recipe. Cooking it in a case of hot water crust pastry is an example of how two different cuisines can come together and create something special and delicious.

Mattar paneer pie

SERVES 6

FOR THE FILLING

2 tablespoons rapeseed oil

1 teaspoon black mustard seeds

1 teaspoon cumin seeds

3 onions, roughly chopped

4 garlic cloves, finely chopped

2.5cm (1 in) fresh root ginger, finely chopped

2 tomatoes, finely chopped

1 teaspoon salt

1 teaspoon chilli powder

1 teaspoon ground cumin

1 teaspoon garam masala

450g (1lb) paneer, cut into small cubes

100g (3½oz) frozen peas, defrosted

20g (¾oz) fresh coriander leaves, finely chopped

FOR THE PASTRY

400g (14oz) plain flour, plus more for dusting

100g (3½oz) strong white bread flour

1 teaspoon ground turmeric

80g (2¾oz) salted butter, chilled and chopped into small cubes

100g (3½oz) white vegetable fat, such as Trex

200ml (7fl oz) water

1 egg, lightly beaten

Start with the filling. In a saucepan, heat the oil, add the mustard and cumin seeds and let them sizzle. Add the onions to the pan and cook over a medium heat for 6–8 minutes until golden. Next, add the garlic and ginger and cook for another minute. Stir in the tomatoes, cover and cook over a low heat for 10 minutes until they have broken down and become soft.

Now add the salt and ground spices, followed by the paneer and the peas and mix well. Take off the heat, mix in the coriander and set aside to cool.

Preheat the oven to 200°C (400°F), Gas Mark 6.

For the pastry, in a bowl, combine both flours and the turmeric and add the butter. Rub the butter into the flour until you get a crumb texture.

Put the vegetable fat and measured water in a saucepan, set over a medium-high heat until it melts together, then bring to the boil. Pour the boiling fat and water mixture into the flour mixture and mix with a wooden spoon. Once it is all combined, knead the dough for a couple of minutes until smooth.

While the dough is still hot, separate one-quarter of it, wrap and set aside. Lightly flour a work surface and roll the rest of the dough out into a big enough circle to line a deep 20cm (8 inch) loose-bottomed round cake tin. Once the tin is lined well with the pastry (push it down into the corners), fill it with the paneer mixture and press it down to make it compact.

Roll the reserved dough into a circle slightly larger than the diameter of the tin, then place it as a lid on top of the paneer filling. Cut off the excess dough from the sides and pinch all around to seal the pie. Make a cut in the centre and brush well with the egg.

Bake for 1 hour until golden.

Leave the pie in the tin for 10 minutes before removing. Serve with a salad or some roast potatoes and my Coriander chutney (see page 195).

Something vegan

Mini saffron cheesecakes

Chocolate, pistachio and cardamom cookies

Peanut meringues

Chocolate, coconut and peanut cake

Almond, coconut and raspberry cake

Lentil potato rolls

Baked crispy okra

Pea and potato sabji stuffed bread

Chutney-topped golden vegetable pizza

Potato curry puffs

Peanut masala tear-and-share rolls

Masala focaccia

Naan with garlicky mushrooms

It might be one of the most expensive spices in the world, but saffron is special; just a pinch of it creates an amazing delicate floral flavour. It is used here with nuts and dates to add richness and vibrancy to a delightful vegan cheesecake.

Mini saffron cheesecakes

MAKES 12

200g (7oz) cashews

125g (4½oz) dates

125g (4½oz) whole almonds

60g (2¼oz) coconut oil, melted, plus more for the tin

2 pinches of saffron threads, plus extra to decorate

100g (3½oz) agave syrup

Soak the cashews in a bowl of warm water for 40 minutes.

In a blender, blitz the dates, then scoop the paste out into a bowl. Now, in the same blender, blitz the almonds until fine, return the dates and blitz together.

Oil a 12-hole cupcake tin and put thin strips of nonstick baking paper in each, to cover the base and come up over opposite sides of each hole. These will help to pull out the cheesecakes when ready. Divide the date-almond mix evenly between the 12 cases, pressing it down with the bottom of a glass. Refrigerate for 30 minutes to set.

Warm 1 tablespoon of coconut oil in a small saucepan and add the saffron. Let it sit for 10 minutes.

Drain the cashews and put them in a clean blender with the remaining coconut oil, soaked saffron and agave syrup. Blitz until smooth. Spoon this mixture on top of the date mix in the cupcake tin. (You may find it helps to use an oiled teaspoon to do this as the mixture is quite sticky.) Place a few saffron threads on top of each and put in the freezer for 3–4 hours until set.

When you are ready to serve, take the tray out of the freezer and use the baking paper strips to pull the cheesecakes from the tin. Put on a serving plate and let sit for 5 minutes before serving, but no longer or they will start losing their shape.

You can store these in the freezer for 2–3 weeks.

When I make a vegan bake, I don't want to compromise on flavour or texture, and these cookies are a lovely example of that. The delicate flavour of cardamom and the richness of dark chocolate and pistachios means these are a riot in every mouthful.

Chocolate, pistachio and cardamom cookies

MAKES 20

120g (4¼oz) vegan butter, softened

170g (6oz) light soft brown sugar

pinch of fine sea salt

275g (9¾oz) plain flour

1½ teaspoons ground cardamom

1 teaspoon baking powder

½ teaspoon bicarbonate of soda

70ml (2½fl oz) almond milk

300g (10½oz) vegan dark chocolate (70 per cent cocoa solids), roughly chopped

60g (2¼oz) pistachios, finely chopped

Preheat the oven to 180°C (350°F), Gas Mark 4. Line 2 baking sheets with nonstick baking paper.

Put the butter in a bowl with the sugar and salt and beat it together with an electric whisk for 2 minutes until smooth and creamy. Sift the plain flour into another bowl with the cardamom, baking powder and bicarbonate of soda and mix it together.

Add the milk to the butter bowl followed by the flour mixture and then the chocolate and pistachios. Fold it all in and bring it together into a soft dough.

Take a lemon-sized portion, shape it into a circle and place on a prepared sheet. Repeat to form all the cookies, leaving enough room between them for the cookies to spread when baked.

Bake for 15 minutes and let them sit on the tray for 2 minutes before transferring to a wire rack.

Store in an airtight container for 3–4 days.

Aquafaba – which simply means "bean water" – is a fabulous ingredient that creates airy meringues without any eggs. Flavoured here with peanuts, topped with coconut yogurt and some beautiful mango to create little individual treats.

Peanut meringues

MAKES 8

50g (1¾oz) peanuts

140ml (5fl oz) aquafaba (you should get this amount from a 400g /14oz can of chickpeas)

140g (5oz) caster sugar, or as needed, plus 4 tablespoons

2 mangoes, stoned, peeled and cut into cubes

300g (10½oz) coconut yogurt

Dry-toast the peanuts in a frying pan for 2 minutes, then crush them in a mortar and pestle into small pieces. Set aside to cool.

Preheat the oven to 120°C (250°F), Gas Mark ½. Line 2 baking sheets with nonstick baking paper.

Drain the chickpeas and measure the liquid from the can (usually 140ml/5fl oz). Use the exact same quantity of sugar for the meringue. Start to whisk the aquafaba on its own, in a clean bowl with an electric whisk, for 6–8 minutes, until it's fluffy and has formed soft peaks. Slowly add the same amount of sugar, 1 tablespoon at a time, while whisking continuously. Now whisk for a further 5 minutes until glossy and stiff.

Spoon 8 portions of meringue from the mixture on to the prepared sheets. Sprinkle some of the peanuts on top and bake for 2 hours, until crispy and dried out. Set aside to cool completely.

In a saucepan, heat the 4 tablespoons of sugar until it starts to turn golden. Add the mangoes and cook over a low heat for 3–4 minutes until they start to soften and slightly change colour.

Place the individual meringues on serving plates, dollop on some coconut yogurt, arrange the mangoes on top, sprinkle with the remaining peanuts and serve immediately.

You can prepare the meringues a day in advance, but only assemble when you are ready to serve.

For me there is only one rule for chocolate cakes: they need to be light, moist and slightly fudgy. This recipe ticks all those boxes. One of the highlights is that, even though it's vegan, you can't really tell, which, for me, means I don't miss the lightness provided by eggs or the creaminess of butter and cream. This cake's creaminess and lightness comes from the peanut butter, coconut milk and almond milk.

Chocolate, coconut and peanut cake

SERVES 8–10

FOR THE CAKE

100g (3½oz) vegan butter, plus more for the tin

300ml (½ pint) almond milk

2 tablespoons cider vinegar

50g (1¾oz) smooth peanut butter

2 teaspoons instant coffee

250g (9oz) self-raising flour

50g (1¾oz) cocoa powder

2 teaspoons baking powder

1 teaspoon bicarbonate of soda

250g (9oz) caster sugar

FOR THE CHOCOLATE CREAM

400ml (14fl oz) can of good-quality, full-fat coconut milk

about 200g (7oz) vegan dark chocolate (70 per cent cocoa solids)

50g (1¾oz) smooth peanut butter

270ml (9½fl oz) vegan cream

50g (1¾oz) icing sugar

Butter 3 x 20cm (8 inch) cake tins with vegan butter and line the bases with nonstick baking paper. Preheat the oven to 180°C (350°F), Gas Mark 4.

Heat the almond milk in a large saucepan and, as soon as the sides start to bubble, take it off the heat. Add the cider vinegar, mix and set aside for a minute, to give it time to split. Then add the butter, peanut butter and coffee and mix well until melted and combined.

In a bowl, combine the flour, cocoa, baking powder, bicarbonate of soda and caster sugar. Now add this to the milk mixture and whisk for 2 minutes until it's smooth and creamy. Divide the batter equally between the 3 cake tins and bake for 30 minutes until a skewer inserted comes out clean. Set aside to cool completely.

Without shaking the can, open the coconut milk and scoop out the solids into a saucepan placed over a set of scales, leaving behind all the liquid. Make a note of the weight, then set over a low heat and gently bring to the boil. Chop up the same weight of chocolate and place it in a heatproof bowl. Pour the hot coconut milk on top and add the peanut butter. Mix well so the chocolate and peanut butter melt, then set aside to cool slightly.

continued overleaf

In another bowl, whip the cream and icing sugar with an electric whisk until you get soft peaks. Add the cooled chocolate cream and whisk until you have a spreadable consistency.

Place a cake on a serving plate and spread over one-third of the chocolate cream. Place another cake on top and repeat until the cake is assembled.

This can be stored in an airtight container in the refrigerator for 4–5 days, just bring it to room temperature before serving.

A simple, elegant cake, equally perfect for an afternoon tea or a big celebration, soft and moist with a slight crunch from the almonds. Coconut cream makes the filling light and fluffy, while the raspberry cardamom jam brings the whole cake together.

Almond, coconut and raspberry cake

SERVES 8–10

FOR THE CAKE

150g (5½oz) vegan butter, plus more for the tins

300ml (½ pint) almond milk

1 tablespoon cider vinegar

225g (8oz) caster sugar

250g (9oz) self-raising flour

50g (1¾oz) ground almonds

1 teaspoon baking powder

1 teaspoon bicarbonate of soda

70g (2½oz) flaked almonds

icing sugar, for dusting

FOR THE FILLING

400ml (14fl oz) can of good-quality, full-fat coconut milk

2 tablespoons caster sugar

4 tablespoons Raspberry cardamom jam (see page 192)

Preheat the oven to 180°C (350°F), Gas Mark 4. Butter and line 2 x 20cm (8 inch) round cake tins.

Put the almond milk in a small bowl and add the vinegar, mix well and let it sit for 5 minutes until the milk curdles.

In another bowl, beat the butter and caster sugar with an electric whisk for a minute until smooth. Add the curdled milk and the rest of the cake ingredients except the flaked almonds. Whisk for another minute, then fold in two-thirds of the flaked almonds.

Divide the mixture between the prepared tins and bake for 30–35 minutes until a skewer inserted comes out clean. Set aside to cool.

Meanwhile, make the filling. Scoop out the thick part of the coconut cream and whisk it, using an electric whisk, with the caster sugar until it forms soft peaks.

Place one cake on a serving plate and spread it with the jam. Spread all the coconut cream on the jam, then top with the second cake.

Dry-toast the remaining almonds in a hot frying pan, stirring constantly, until lightly golden. Tip them out on to a plate to stop the cooking and let cool.

Sprinkle the cooled almonds on top of the cake, dust with icing sugar and serve immediately.

This can be stored in an airtight container in the refrigerator for 3–4 days, just bring it to room temperature before serving.

Rolls are such an easy snack to prepare for lunchboxes, picnics, party snacks or just for something to enjoy in the middle of the day. My son is more than happy with these for dinner. The filling is a combination of lentils that add a bite, soft potatoes and some cheese, all deliciously balanced with a lovely hit of spices.

Lentil potato rolls

MAKES 10

1 tablespoon sunflower oil

1 onion, finely chopped

2 garlic cloves, finely chopped

400g (14oz) can of green lentils in water, drained and rinsed

½ teaspoon salt

½ teaspoon chilli powder

1 teaspoon chaat masala

1 medium potato, boiled and mashed

60g (2¼oz) vegan cheese

320g (11¼oz) pack of ready-rolled vegan puff pastry

1 tablespoon almond milk, or any other vegan milk

1 tablespoon tamari

Coriander chutney (see page 195), to serve

Put the oil in a saucepan, and, once hot, add the onion. Cook for 5 minutes over a medium heat until softened. Now add the garlic and cook for another minute.

Add the lentils and cook for 2 more minutes, then stir in the salt and spices and transfer to a bowl to cool. Add the potato and cheese and mix well.

Preheat the oven to 200°C (400°F), Gas Mark 6. Line 2 baking sheets with nonstick baking paper.

Unroll the pastry and fill the centre lengthways with a line of the cooled filling. Brush one side with the milk and fold it to the centre, on top of the filling. Brush more milk on the other side of the pastry, seal to make a secure roll, then cut this into 10 pieces. Place them on the prepared trays, cut-sides down.

Brush them with tamari and bake for 25–30 minutes until golden.

Serve them warm and crispy with some coriander chutney, if liked.

Crispy okra is a popular Indian dish. Not only can you find it being cooked in Indian homes, but it's also a very popular side dish in restaurants, usually deep-fried in hot oil until crispy and golden. Here I have made it as a lovely baked snack that you can enjoy with some chai or any other drink.

Baked crispy okra

SERVES 4

500g (1lb 2oz) okra, washed and dried

50g (1¾oz) gram flour

½ teaspoon fine sea salt

½ teaspoon chilli powder

1 teaspoon ground cumin

1 teaspoon chaat masala

3 tablespoons rapeseed oil

Very spicy apple chutney (see page 198), to serve

Preheat the oven to 200°C (400°F), Gas Mark 6.

Cut off the heads and tails of the okra and slice them into thin long pieces.

In a bowl, combine all the dry ingredients and mix well. Put the oil into another bowl.

Coat the okra pieces in the oil, then roll them in the bowl of dry ingredients.

Place the okra on a baking tray and bake for 20–25 minutes until golden and crispy. Enjoy them fresh and hot with some chutney on the side.

The potato and pea filling here is a delicious vegan sabji, usually enjoyed with dal and rice or flatbreads, or used to fill samosas. I use it to make a beautiful stuffed loaf, like a ready-baked sandwich. The bread is soft and light, packed with flavour and finished with garlicky coriander oil: a meal in itself.

Pea and potato sabji stuffed bread

MAKES 2 LOAVES

FOR THE BREAD

400g (14oz) strong white bread flour, plus more for dusting

7g (¼oz) fine sea salt

7g (¼oz) fast-action dried yeast

1 teaspoon caster sugar

1 teaspoon carom seeds (ajwain)

230ml (8¼fl oz) water, or as needed

a little neutral-tasting oil

FOR THE FILLING

2 tablespoons sunflower oil

1 teaspoon mustard seeds

1 teaspoon cumin seeds

1 red onion, finely chopped

1 bird's eye green chilli, finely chopped

½ teaspoon salt

½ teaspoon chilli powder

1 teaspoon garam masala

1 teaspoon ground turmeric

2 medium potatoes, peeled and cut into 1cm (½ inch) pieces

200g (7oz) frozen peas

FOR THE OIL

50ml (1¾fl oz) extra virgin olive oil

5 garlic cloves, finely chopped

10g (¼oz) fresh coriander leaves, finely chopped

Mix the flour, salt, yeast, sugar and carom seeds in the bowl of a food mixer fitted with the dough hook, or just in a large bowl. Slowly add the measured water and bring it together into a soft dough. You might not need all the water, or you may need a bit more. Knead for 8 minutes until smooth and stretchy. Oil a bowl and put the dough in it, then cover and let it prove for 1–2 hours or until doubled in size.

Meanwhile, prepare the filling. Heat the oil in a pan, add the mustard and cumin seeds and let them sizzle. Add the onion and cook for 5 minutes until softened, then add the green chilli and cook for another minute. Next, add the salt and spices, followed by the potatoes. Add 2 tablespoons of water, cover and cook for 10 minutes over a low heat. Now add the peas, cover and cook for another 5–8 minutes until the potatoes are tender. Set aside to cool completely.

Divide the dough in half. Roll out one portion into a long 30 x 25cm (12 x 10 inch) oval and place half the pea mixture in the middle of it. With a sharp knife, make 2.5cm- (1 inch-) long diagonal cuts on either side of the filling like wings, leaving the top

continued overleaf

and bottom parts of the dough whole. Fold the top and bottom parts over the filling, then start overlapping the right- and left-hand pieces alternately, sealing the filling inside. Transfer the loaf to a floured baking tray, then repeat to stuff and shape the second loaf. Cover and let them prove for 1 hour.

Meanwhile put the oil, garlic and coriander in a bowl and let it infuse.

Preheat the oven to 200°C (400°F), Gas Mark 6. Bake the breads for 25 minutes, or until golden. Once baked, brush the infused oil over the loaves and let them cool down before serving.

Wrap the loaves up well and eat within a day.

When I say pizza you might think of cheesy toppings, but this is not the usual version. I have made a regular pizza base, spread it with my very own tomato chutney with stunning deep flavours and topped it with cooked golden vegetables. The base is a lovely wholesome, flavourful bread that I hope you will enjoy as much as I do.

Chutney-topped golden vegetable pizza

MAKES 4

FOR THE DOUGH

400g (14oz) strong white bread flour, plus more for dusting

7g (¼oz) fine sea salt

7g (¼oz) fast-action dried yeast

275–300ml (9½–10fl oz) water

a little olive oil

FOR THE TOPPING

2 tablespoons olive oil

1 courgette, finely sliced

1 small aubergine, finely sliced

1 red onion, finely sliced

8–12 tablespoons Spiced tomato chutney (see page 193)

pinch of salt

pinch of freshly ground black pepper

Put the flour, salt and yeast in a bowl and slowly add the water. Stop adding the water once you have a soft dough. Knead it in a food mixer fitted with the dough hook, or by hand on a floured surface, for 8 minutes, until it's elastic and smooth. Put some olive oil in a bowl and put the dough in it. Cover and let it prove for 1–2 hours or until doubled in size.

Divide the dough into 4 portions and shape each into a ball, folding it quite tightly. Place on a very well-floured baking tray. Cover and let it rest for 1 hour, or until doubled in size once more.

Meanwhile, for the topping, heat a frying pan and add the oil. Cook the courgette for 2 minutes on each side until lightly golden, then remove the slices to a plate. Cook the aubergine for 2–3 minutes on each side and remove it to the same plate. Now cook the onion in the same pan for 6–8 minutes until golden.

Preheat the oven to 220°C (425°F), Gas Mark 7.

On a lightly floured surface, roll out each portion of dough into a big circle, roughly 15–20cm (6–8 inches) in diameter. Spread each with 2–3 tablespoons of tomato chutney and arrange the lightly golden vegetables on top with a pinch each of salt and pepper.

Place the pizzas in the hot oven and bake for 12–15 minutes, or until golden and crispy. Serve hot.

You will find many variations of curry puffs from different parts of the world. Though, where I come from, they are not called curry puffs; instead, we call them vegetable patties. In this recipe I use only potatoes, instead of mixed vegetables. The curry powder is the main flavour, marrying well with the coconut cream, while puff pastry is the perfect carrier for this delicious filling. Try serving warm with some Chilli chutney (see page 199) for extra heat.

Potato curry puffs

MAKES 8

2 tbsp sunflower oil

2 medium-sized onions, finely chopped

1 leek, finely chopped

¾ teaspoon salt

1 teaspoon chilli powder

2 tablespoons mild curry powder

2 medium-sized potatoes (roughly 500g/1lb 2oz in total), peeled and cut into 1.5cm (⅝ inch) pieces

160ml (5½fl oz) can of coconut cream

2 x 320g (11¼oz) pack of ready-rolled vegan puff pastry

plain flour, for dusting

2 tablespoons almond milk, or any other vegan milk, for brushing the puffs

Heat the oil in a pan, add the onions and cook for 5 minutes until softened. Next, add the leek and cook for another 5 minutes over a low heat. Add the salt, chilli and curry powders, followed by the potatoes, and mix well. Now add the coconut cream, cover and let it cook over a low heat for 10 minutes until the potatoes are done and there is no liquid remaining. Let it cool completely.

Preheat the oven to 200°C (400°F), Gas Mark 6. Line 2 baking trays with nonstick baking paper.

Unroll each sheet of puff pastry on a lightly floured work surface and roll them out to an additional 2.5cm (1 inch) bigger on all sides. Cut each pastry sheet into 4 equal circles, or rectangles, if you prefer. Fill half the circles or rectangles with the cooled potatoes, brush milk on the edges, then fold the unfilled half of the pastry over the filling and crimp the edges. Brush with milk and place on the prepared trays.

Bake for 30–35 minutes until golden and crisp. Serve warm.

Tear-and-share bread is a good idea when cooking for family or friends, as you just make one and everyone can help themselves. If you are one of those bread lovers who would just eat any bread on its own, or with butter, or dipped in olive oil, or with a chutney, this will make you very happy. It has layers of peanut masala rolled into it. Enjoy it warm or slice a portion in half and make a sandwich.

Peanut masala tear-and-share rolls

SERVES 6–8

FOR THE BREAD

400g (14oz) strong white bread flour

1 teaspoon caster sugar

1¼ teaspoons fine sea salt

7g (¼oz) fast-action dried yeast

3 teaspoons extra virgin olive oil, plus more for glazing

250ml (9fl oz) water, or as needed

neutral-tasting oil, for the tin

FOR THE FILLING

100g (3½oz) peanuts

2 tablespoons gram flour

1 green chilli, finely chopped

20g (¾oz) fresh coriander leaves, finely chopped

1 teaspoon salt

1 teaspoon ground turmeric

1 teaspoon ground cumin

1 teaspoon ground coriander

4 tablespoons tomato purée

2 tablespoons extra virgin olive oil

4 tablespoons water

Put the flour, sugar and salt in a bowl and mix. Add the yeast and 2 teaspoons of the olive oil and stir it in. Slowly add the measured water, mixing well until you get a soft dough. You might not need all the water, or you may need a bit more. Knead for 8–10 minutes, either by hand or in a food mixer fitted with the dough hook.

Use the remaining 1 teaspoon of olive oil to coat a large bowl. Place the dough in it, cover and prove for 1–2 hours, until doubled in size.

To prepare the filling, dry-toast the peanuts in a pan for 2 minutes over a medium heat until golden and properly toasted. Tip them into a mortar and pestle and crush until broken up but not too fine. In the same pan, dry-toast the gram flour over a low heat for a couple of minutes until a light golden colour. Put this in a bowl with the peanuts and the rest of the filling ingredients and mix.

Turn the dough out onto a clean work surface and knead for a few seconds. Roll it out into a rectangle measuring about 40 x 30cm (16 x 12 inches). Spread over the peanut masala then roll it up from a long side as tightly as possible. Cut the roll into 12 equal pieces.

Oil a 25cm (10 inch) round springform cake tin. Place the dough pieces in the tin, cover and prove for 1 hour or until doubled in size.

Preheat the oven to 200°C (400°F), Gas Mark 6. Bake for 30–35 minutes until golden. Brush the bread with extra virgin olive oil and leave it in the tin for 10 minutes before removing.

Best served warm or at room temperature on the day it is made.

This bread enjoys an olive oil bath and is good enough to enjoy on its own. I haven't met anyone who doesn't like focaccia, and as it's so versatile, this is one bread we should all make at home. Here I have given the bread a bit of a kick with some spicy masala to wake it from its olive oil bath. Tear it into pieces and enjoy little bursts of flavour with every bite.

Masala focaccia

SERVES 4–6

FOR THE FOCACCIA

500g (1lb 2oz) strong white bread flour

10g (¼oz) fine sea salt

10g (¼oz) fast-action dried yeast

380–400ml (13–14fl oz) water

100ml (3½fl oz) extra virgin olive oil

FOR THE MASALA

2 tablespoons sunflower oil

2 medium onions, finely chopped

1 bird's eye green chilli, finely chopped

2.5cm (1 inch) fresh root ginger, finely chopped

5 garlic cloves, finely chopped

2 medium tomatoes, finely chopped

½ teaspoon chilli powder

¼ teaspoon salt

TO FINISH

pinch of sea salt flakes

2 tablespoons extra virgin olive oil

Put the flour, salt and yeast in the bowl of a food mixer fitted with the dough hook – or just in a bowl and work by hand – and slowly add the measured water, starting with the smaller amount. The dough should be slightly sticky, so don't add extra flour. Knead it for 8–10 minutes until the dough is stretchy and smooth, it will still be sticky so don't worry.

Put around 80ml (2¾fl oz) of the olive oil in a deep plastic box or a bowl and swirl it all around to spread it evenly, making sure the whole container is well oiled so the dough doesn't stick. Now transfer the dough to the oily container, cover and let it prove for 2 hours or until doubled in size.

Meanwhile, prepare the masala. Heat the sunflower oil in a frying pan over a medium heat, add the onions and cook for 8–10 minutes until deep golden. Next, add the chilli, ginger and garlic and cook for another minute. Add the tomatoes and cook for another 8–10 minutes until they have softened and the masala has reduced and come together nicely. Add the chilli powder and salt, mix well, then set aside to cool.

continued overleaf

Put the remaining 4 teaspoons of olive oil in a traybake tin measuring around 30 x 20 x 4–5cm (12 x 8 x 2 inches). Make sure to brush the oil around the whole tin. Now carefully transfer the dough into the prepared tin. Using your fingers, gently stretch the dough so it covers the whole tin. Cover the dough and let it prove for 1 hour.

Preheat the oven to 220°C (425°F), Gas Mark 7. Use your fingers to press into the dough, making hollows all over. Spoon the cooled masala into the holes, then sprinkle with sea salt and bake for 25 minutes until golden and baked.

Drizzle the 2 tablespoons of extra virgin olive oil on top and let the focaccia sit in the tin for a few minutes before serving.

Best eaten on the day but will keep for 2–3.

The naan I usually make is one that I learned from my mum, which uses yogurt and sometimes milk, but this vegan naan is a very lovely thing. Here chutney forms a base for the mushrooms, and, finished with a hint of coconut, chilli and onions, it is beautiful. Feel free to substitute the mushrooms for any vegan topping – cauliflower, potatoes, lentils or aubergine would all work well.

Naan with garlicky mushrooms

MAKES 6

FOR THE NAAN

200g (7oz) strong white bread flour, plus more for dusting

100g (3½oz) plain flour

1 teaspoon fast-action dried yeast

½ teaspoon fine sea salt

½ teaspoon caster sugar

180ml (6fl oz) water, or as needed

FOR THE MUSHROOMS

2 tablespoons rapeseed oil, plus more for brushing the naan

6 garlic cloves, finely sliced

1 red chilli, finely sliced

500g (1lb 2oz) chestnut mushrooms, finely sliced

½ teaspoon dark soy sauce

½ teaspoon chilli garlic sauce

¼ teaspoon fine sea salt

10g (¼oz) fresh coriander leaves, finely chopped

TO SERVE

2 red onions, finely sliced

¼ teaspoon fine sea salt, plus more for the onions

1 teaspoon chilli flakes, plus more for sprinkling

juice of ½ lemon

6 tablespoons coconut yogurt

1 teaspoon ground cumin

Coriander chutney (see page 195)

Put the flours, yeast, salt and sugar in a bowl, mix well and slowly add the water. You might not need all the water, or you may need a bit more. Knead for 8–10 minutes until smooth and stretchy. Place in a bowl, cover and let rest for 1–2 hours until doubled in size.

Heat the oil in a saucepan, add the garlic and cook for a few seconds until it starts to turn golden. Next, add the chilli and then the mushrooms and cook for 5–6 minutes over a high heat until soft and all the liquid has evaporated. Remove from the heat, add the soy sauce, chilli sauce, salt and coriander, mix well and set aside.

Put the sliced red onions in a bowl, add a pinch of salt, the chilli flakes and lemon juice and mix well.

In a separate bowl, mix the coconut yogurt, salt and cumin.

Divide the dough into 6 portions. Heat a large flat frying pan. Roll each portion on a well-floured work surface into a large circle 20–25cm (8–10 inches) in diameter. It will be nice and thin. Cook in the hot pan for 1–2 minutes on each side until golden.

Brush some rapeseed oil on top, spread over some coriander chutney, spoon on some mushrooms and red onions, drizzle with yogurt and sprinkle with chilli flakes. Roll up loosely and serve immediately. Repeat to cook, top and roll all the naans.

You can prepare all components separately a few hours in advance and put this together just before serving.

Something small

Anise and walnut rugelach

Coconut and lime cookies

Jaggery coconut baklava

Shortbread with cardamom caramel

Coffee and chocolate lamingtons

Anise doughnuts

Rose and cardamom yum yums

Lemon, poppy seed and raspberry cupcakes

Black tahini and cream cheese cookies

Cardamom pistachio buns

Coffee cream profiteroles with chocolate

Matcha and strawberry sponge fingers

Chocolate-coffee scones

Mini caramel and hazelnut meringue cakes

Our favourite cookies

For me, the best way to describe these would be to say that they are pastry biscuits: crunchy but short due to the butter and with a nutty filling, all in all a delicious little bite with a warm anise flavour.

Anise and walnut rugelach

MAKES 16

FOR THE RUGELACH

150g (5½oz) plain flour, plus more for dusting

pinch of fine sea salt

1 teaspoon ground star anise

¼ teaspoon baking powder

120g (4¼oz) unsalted butter, chilled and chopped into small cubes

120g (4¼oz) full-fat cream cheese

2 tablespoons lemon juice

1 egg, lightly beaten

FOR THE FILLING

100g (3½oz) hazelnuts

75g (2¾oz) light soft brown sugar

50g (1¾oz) walnuts, blitzed to a rough powder

¼ teaspoon ground cinnamon

Put the flour, salt, anise and baking powder in a bowl and mix together. Add the butter and rub it into the flour until you get a crumb texture. Mix in the cream cheese until you get a soft dough.

Lightly flour a work surface and knead the dough for a few seconds. Divide into 2 portions, flatten each slightly, cover and chill in the refrigerator for 1 hour.

Line 2 baking trays with nonstick baking paper.

Dry-roast the hazelnuts in a pan for 2 minutes over a medium heat until golden and properly toasted. Tip them into a mortar and pestle and crush until broken up but not too fine. Combine with the rest of the filling ingredients in a bowl.

Roll out one portion of the dough on a lightly floured surface to a 30cm (12 inch) circle. Brush with lemon juice and sprinkle over half the filling. Using a sharp knife, cut the circle into 8 equal triangles. Now start rolling each portion from the outside arc towards the narrow bit of the triangle. Place them on the prepared trays. Repeat with the other dough portion. Leave the trays in the refrigerator to chill for 30 minutes.

Preheat the oven to 200°C (400°F), Gas Mark 6. Brush the rugelach with egg and bake for 20–25 minutes until golden and crispy. Leave on the trays for 5 minutes, then transfer to a wire rack to cool.

These are best enjoyed fresh, but any leftovers can be stored in an airtight container for 1–2 days.

These little cookie treats are a lovely combination of zesty lime and chewy coconut, all of which comes together with the chocolate both within and on top of the cookies. You can even try dipping them in white chocolate or some caramel, if you like.

Coconut and lime cookies

MAKES 18–20

FOR THE COOKIES

100g (3½oz) unsalted butter, softened

100g (3½oz) caster sugar

50g (1¾oz) dark chocolate (70 per cent cocoa solids)

20g (¾oz) creamed coconut, grated

finely grated zest of 1 lime, plus 1 tablespoon lime juice

40g (1½oz) desiccated coconut

220g (7¾oz) plain flour

FOR THE ICING

50g (1¾oz) dark chocolate (70 per cent cocoa solids)

30g (1oz) unsalted butter

2 tablespoons desiccated coconut

Preheat the oven to 180°C (350°F), Gas Mark 4. Line 2 baking trays with nonstick baking paper.

Beat the butter and sugar with an electric whisk for 2 minutes until light and creamy. Break the chocolate into a heatproof bowl and set it over a saucepan of simmering water until melted (make sure the bowl does not touch the water), then remove from the heat. Add the creamed coconut, lime zest and juice to the sugar and butter mixture and mix well. Add the desiccated coconut, flour and the cooled, melted chocolate and bring it together into a soft dough. Knead until smooth.

Take a lime-sized portion of the dough, shape it into a ball, then flatten it slightly. Repeat with the remaining dough. Place on the prepared trays and bake for 15 minutes. Transfer to a wire rack to cool completely.

Meanwhile, make the icing. Break the chocolate into a heatproof bowl, add the butter and set it over a saucepan of simmering water until melted (make sure the bowl does not touch the water). Dip one side of the biscuits in the chocolate and sprinkle coconut on top. Set aside to set, then serve.

Store them in an airtight container for 3–4 days.

The flavour of jaggery is unique: though it's just unrefined sugar it has a deep caramel flavour. It's used a lot in Indian sweets, as well as eaten on its own as a side dish with savoury food. In this baklava I use jaggery in the syrup: it goes really well with nuts and coconut, bringing a different mix to the regular baklava flavours.

Jaggery coconut baklava

MAKES 20–25

FOR THE BAKLAVA

40g (1½oz) cashews

40g (1½oz) pistachios

40g (1½oz) desiccated coconut

220g (7¾oz) pack of filo pastry (12 sheets)

150g (5½oz) unsalted butter, melted

FOR THE SYRUP

100g (3½oz) jaggery, cut into small pieces

200ml (7fl oz) water

200g (7oz) golden granulated sugar

Put the cashews, pistachios and coconut in a blender or food processor and blitz it together to make a slightly coarse mix.

Preheat the oven to 180°C (350°F), Gas Mark 4.

Take a rectanglular baking tin, measuring roughly 30 x 18cm (12 x 7 inches) and place a sheet of filo in it. Brush it generously with melted butter. Repeat to layer in and butter 4 filo sheets in total. Sprinkle in half the nutty filling, then layer in and butter 4 more sheets of filo. Sprinkle in the other half of the filling and layer with the remaining 4 sheets of filo, again buttering each one generously.

Bake for 35–40 minutes until golden and crispy.

Meanwhile, prepare the syrup. Put the jaggery, measured water and granulated sugar in a saucepan and bring to the boil, then reduce the heat and cook over a low heat for 6–8 minutes. Remove from the heat.

Once the baklava is baked, cut it into small bite-sized diamonds with a sharp knife. Evenly pour the warm syrup over the top, making sure every piece is soaked. Let it sit for a few hours, or overnight, so the pastry can soak up all the syrup.

Store in an airtight container for 3–4 days.

These are so light, crumbly and delicious. To make them even more special, I have sandwiched them with cardamom-flavoured salted caramel, though you could use jam or chocolate spread, if you like.

Shortbread with cardamom caramel

MAKES 10

300g (10½oz) plain flour

70g (2½oz) icing sugar

180g (6oz) unsalted butter, softened

1 large egg, lightly beaten

1 teaspoon ground cardamom

1 quantity Salted caramel sauce (see page 189)

Put the flour and icing sugar in a bowl and mix well. Next, add the butter and rub it in until you have crumbs. Now add the egg and bring the dough together. Wrap the shortbread in clingfilm and put it in the refrigerator for 15–20 minutes.

Preheat the oven to 180°C (350°F), Gas Mark 4. Line 2 baking sheets with nonstick baking paper.

Put the dough on another sheet of baking paper and roll it out into a thin sheet, 2–3mm (1/8 inch) thick. Now take a 6cm (2½ inch) round cookie cutter, cut the dough into circles and put them on the prepared baking sheets. Bring the leftover dough together, roll it out again and cut more circles. You should get around 20 biscuits.

Bake for 15 minutes until golden, then set aside to cool completely.

Stir the cardamom into the caramel sauce, then spoon it into a piping bag. Pipe some caramel on a biscuit and top with another biscuit to make a sandwich. Repeat to sandwich all the biscuits.

These can be stored in an airtight container for 2–3 days.

I will never forget the flavour of the absolutely delicious lamingtons that I enjoyed in Australia. We were staying on Hamilton Island and they served fresh-baked lamingtons on their breakfast menu. Guess what I had for breakfast the whole time we stayed there? Yes, these soft, coconutty cake bites. Here I have added an extra coffee flavour to kick-start my day in an even better way!

Coffee and chocolate lamingtons

MAKES 24

FOR THE CAKE

30g (1oz) unsalted butter, plus more for the tin

200g (7oz) golden caster sugar

4 large eggs

2 tablespoons whole milk

2 tablespoons instant coffee granules

200g (7oz) self-raising flour

¼ teaspoon fine sea salt

FOR THE COATING

200g (7oz) desiccated coconut

80g (2¾oz) unsalted butter, melted

250ml (9fl oz) whole milk

60g (2¼oz) cocoa powder

400g (14oz) icing sugar, sifted

Preheat the oven to 180°C (350°F), Gas Mark 4 and butter a 30 x 20cm (12 x 8 inch) rectangular cake tin and line it with nonstick baking paper.

Put the sugar and eggs in the bowl of a food mixer fitted with the whisk attachment. Whisk for 6 minutes, or until the mixture is light and fluffy and leaves a ribbon of batter when you lift the whisk.

Meanwhile, warm the milk, butter and coffee in a saucepan until the butter has melted and coffee has dissolved. Let this cool for a bit.

Add the flour and salt to the eggs and gently fold in without losing any air. Now drizzle the coffee mix on top and fold that in too.

Pour this batter into the prepared tin and bake for 25 minutes until a skewer inserted comes out clean. After 5 minutes, remove it from the tin to a wire rack to cool completely. Cut into 24 squares. It will be easier to coat the lamingtons if you chill the squares overnight.

Put the coconut in a wide bowl. Pour the melted butter into a another big bowl, add the milk and whisk well. To this, add the cocoa powder, then the icing sugar. Whisk until smooth and glossy.

Take one cake square at a time, and, with the help of 2 forks, dip it into the cocoa mix on all sides, then drop it into the coconut. Turn it around so that it is covered. Set aside to set, then serve.

Store in an airtight container for 3–4 days.

This is a very special recipe for me and will always be close to my heart. These delicious, melt-in-your-mouth doughnuts are inspired by my friend Luis, who I met in the *Bake Off* tent many years ago. He spoke about these doughnuts. When filming was over, we all met for a big get-together. Luis walked in with a massive box of these doughnuts, three of which I devoured... and I would have eaten more if I could. Sadly Luis is no longer with us, but his love of food will always be remembered and so will these absolutely amazing doughnuts.

Anise doughnuts

MAKES 20

130ml (4¼fl oz) extra virgin olive oil

3 tablespoons aniseeds

400g (14oz) plain flour, plus more for dusting

3 large eggs, lightly beaten

140g (5oz) golden caster sugar, plus 200g (7oz) more for coating

8g (¼oz) baking powder

50ml (1¾fl oz) aniseed liqueur (I use sambuca)

sunflower oil, for deep-frying

Put the oil and aniseeds in a saucepan. Cook over a low heat for 5 minutes until the seeds become golden. Set aside to infuse and cool.

In a bowl, combine the flour, eggs, 140g (5oz) of sugar, the baking powder and liqueur. Put a fine-meshed sieve over the bowl and pour in the aniseed-infused oil (discard the seeds). Combine it well until you have a thick and sticky dough.

Generously flour a few baking trays so that the doughnuts don't stick to them. Flour your hands well, too. Shape a portion of dough, roughly the size of a lime, into a ball. Make a hole in the middle and place it on a prepared tray. Repeat to form all the doughnuts.

Put the 200g (7oz) of sugar into a bowl. Line a large plate with several sheets of kitchen paper.

Pour the sunflower oil into a deep saucepan to a depth of one-third (or use a deep-fat fryer and follow the manufacturer's instructions). Heat the oil over a medium heat to 170°C (340°F). Fry the doughnuts in the order you shaped them, using a well-floured spatula to lift them and carefully place them in the hot oil, 1–2 at a time, so as not to overcrowd the pan. Fry them for a couple of minutes on each side, turning once carefully with the spatula, until golden. Remove them on to the kitchen paper, then transfer to the bowl of caster sugar and roll to coat completely.

Enjoy these fresh, though they keep really well in an airtight container for 3–4 days.

The whole idea of soft, bread-like doughnuts covered with a thin layer of icing just pleasantly surprised me when I tried yum yums for the first time, and I loved them. I do tend to buy them whenever I spot them in a bakery, which is not very often. So I make my own, adding the sweetness of cardamom which pairs really well with fragrant rose in the icing.

Rose and cardamom yum yums

MAKES 24

300g (10½oz) strong white bread flour, plus more for dusting

7g (¼oz) fast-action dried yeast

½ teaspoon fine sea salt

20g (¾oz) caster sugar

1 teaspoon ground cardamom

50g (1¾oz) unsalted butter, chilled and chopped into small cubes

1 large egg

160ml (5½fl oz) water, plus 3 tablespoons

200g (7oz) icing sugar

1 teaspoon rosewater

sunflower oil, for deep-frying

Put the flour, yeast, salt, sugar and cardamom in a large bowl and mix well. To this add the cubed butter and just mix it in so that all the butter is coated; you don't need to rub the butter in on this occasion.

Mix the egg and measured 160ml (5½fl oz) water in a bowl. Slowly pour this into the flour bowl, mixing it together until you get a soft dough (you may not need all of the water). Cover and let it rest for 30 minutes.

On a lightly floured work surface, roll out the dough into a rectangle, roughly 25 x 12.5cm (10 x 5 inches). Fold one-quarter of the pastry – from a short side – over the rest, then do the same with the other short side. Now fold both together. You will have a pastry stack of 4 layers on the work surface. Turn it by 90° clockwise, then roll out once more into a 25 x 12.5cm (10 x 5 inches) rectangle. Repeat 3 times. Cover and let the dough rest in the refrigerator for 30 minutes.

Roll out the dough on a lightly floured work surface into a rectangle, roughly 30 x 20cm (12 x 8 inches). Cut the rectangle in half lengthways. Cut each of these rectangles into 12 strips. You should be left with 24 strips roughly 10 x 2.5cm (4 x 1 inches).

Generously flour a few baking trays. Take each strip and cut in half lengthways, keeping the top bit together to give you two 'legs'. Twist these legs together, then seal with a pinch. Place the yum yums on the prepared trays, cover and let prove for 1 hour.

Meanwhile, combine the icing sugar, 3 tablespoons of water and rosewater in a bowl and whisk until smooth.

Line a large plate with several sheets of kitchen paper.

Pour the sunflower oil into a deep saucepan to a depth of one-third (or use a deep-fat fryer and follow the manufacturer's instructions). Heat the oil over a medium heat to 170°C (340°F). Use a well-floured spatula to lift and carefully place the yum yums in the hot oil, 1–2 at a time, so as not to overcrowd the pan. Fry for 1 minute on each side, turning once with the spatula, until golden. Put them on the kitchen paper and immediately brush generously with the icing.

Repeat to fry and ice all the yum yums. Leave to cool completely before serving.

These are best enjoyed fresh, but any leftovers can be stored in an airtight container for 1–2 days.

The tartness of the curd filling these poppy seed cupcakes, topped with fresh raspberry cream, means these wonderful cupcakes are not very hard to sell! The basic recipe can be filled with the lovely Salted caramel sauce (see page 189), or add any other filling of your choice and make them your own.

Lemon, poppy seed and raspberry cupcakes

MAKES 12

FOR THE CUPCAKES

125g (4½oz) unsalted butter, softened

125g (4½oz) golden caster sugar

2 large eggs

125g (4½oz) self-raising flour

½ teaspoon vanilla extract

1 tablespoon milk

1 teaspoon black poppy seeds

FOR THE ICING

½ portion Lemon and passion fruit curd (see page 188)

200ml (7fl oz) double cream

100g (3½oz) full-fat cream cheese

2 tablespoons caster sugar

200g (7oz) raspberries

Preheat the oven to 180°C (350°F), Gas Mark 4. Line a 12-hole cupcake tin with cupcake liners.

In a bowl, combine all the cupcake ingredients together and whisk with an electric whisk for 2 minutes until creamy and pale. Spoon this into the prepared cupcake liners and bake for 20 minutes. Remove the cupcakes from the tin immediately and leave them on a wire rack to cool completely.

With a sharp knife or an apple corer, make a small hole in the middle of each cooled cupcake. (Discard or, better still, eat the cake you remove.) Put a teaspoonful of passion fruit curd in each hole.

In another bowl, whip the cream, cream cheese and sugar until the mixture forms soft peaks. Break up half the raspberries into the cream and fold them in. Now, using a palette knife, put the icing on top of the cakes (you can also use a piping bag) and finish with the remaining raspberries on top.

Store any leftover cupcakes in the refrigerator for 2 days, but return to room temperature before serving.

This might sound unusual, but the nutty, earthy flavour of sesame with cream cheese and chocolate is so, so good. The cream cheese makes them less sweet and the black tahini adds a depth of colour, though you can use regular tahini as well if that is what you have at hand. These are best enjoyed still slightly warm.

Black tahini and cream cheese cookies

MAKES 15–17

120g (4½oz) unsalted butter, softened

80g (2¾oz) dark brown muscovado sugar

60g (2¼oz) caster sugar

1 teaspoon vanilla extract

1 large egg

180g (6¼oz) plain flour

½ teaspoon bicarbonate of soda

2 tablespoons black tahini

100g (3½oz) dark chocolate (70 per cent cocoa solids), roughly chopped

170g (5¾oz) full-fat cream cheese

1 tablespoon black sesame seeds

In a bowl and using an electric whisk, beat the butter and sugars for a minute until creamy and smooth. Add the vanilla and egg and whisk until combined.

Now add the flour, bicarbonate of soda, tahini and chocolate and combine it well. Cover and leave it to set in the refrigerator for 15 minutes.

Preheat the oven to 180°C (350°F), Gas Mark 4. Line 2 baking trays with nonstick baking paper.

Take a spoonful of cookie dough about the size of a lime, shape into a ball and place on a prepared tray. Press it down slightly, then dollop 1 teaspoon of cream cheese on top and sprinkle with sesame seeds. Repeat with the rest of the dough, leaving space between each cookie for them to spread.

Bake for 15 minutes, then transfer to a wire rack to set. These are best enjoyed straight after baking, but can be stored in an airtight container for 2 days.

A warm, fresh bun just out of the oven, sticky from sugar syrup and filled with a sweet, fragrant, nutty filling. These are divine and best enjoyed with a masala chai or a good cup of coffee. Once you have tried these buns, you can experiment with the filling, using different sugars, nuts or even adding chocolate.

Cardamom pistachio buns

MAKES 24

FOR THE DOUGH

200ml (7fl oz) whole milk, plus more if needed

1 teaspoon ground cardamom

175g (6oz) unsalted butter, chopped into small cubes, plus more for the tins

300g (10½oz) strong white bread flour, plus more for dusting

300g (10½oz) plain flour

10g (¼oz) fine sea salt

10g (¼oz) fast-action dried yeast

60g (2¼oz) golden caster sugar

2 large eggs, lightly beaten, plus 1 more, to glaze

FOR THE FILLING

150g (5½oz) unsalted butter, softened

200g (7oz) light soft brown sugar

1 teaspoon ground cinnamon

1 teaspoon ground cardamom

100g (3½oz) pistachios, blitzed to a fine powder, plus more for the topping

FOR THE SYRUP

100g (3½oz) caster sugar

100ml (3½fl oz) water

Pour the milk into a saucepan and warm over a medium heat until hot to touch. Add the cardamom and butter, remove from the heat and set aside to melt.

Put the flours into the bowl of a food mixer fitted with the dough hook. Add the salt, yeast and sugar and mix well, then add the 2 eggs. Slowly pour in the milk to bring the dough together until soft. You might not need it all, or you may need a bit more. Knead for 8 minutes until smooth and stretchy. Put in a bowl, cover and let prove for a couple of hours, or until doubled in size.

In another bowl, whisk the butter, sugar, cinnamon and cardamom with an electric whisk for a minute until creamy and smooth.

Roll out the dough on a work surface lightly dusted with flour into a rectangle, roughly 50 x 30cm (20 x 12 inches), making sure a longer side is facing you.

Spread with the butter mix, then sprinkle over the ground pistachios, pressing them down into the butter.

Fold the top three-quarters down, then fold the bottom one-quarter on top of that, like an envelope. Cut this long rectangle into 24 thin strips.

Butter 2 x 12-hole cupcake tins. Take each strip and, keeping the top together, cut each one in half lengthways. Twist these pieces together and press the ends to seal. Coil into a bun shape and place in the prepared tin. Repeat to form all the buns, then cover and let them prove for 1 hour.

Preheat the oven to 190°C (375°F), Gas Mark 5. Brush the buns with beaten egg, sprinkle with pistachios and bake for 20 minutes until golden.

Meanwhile, prepare the syrup by putting the sugar and measured water in a saucepan and bringing to the boil. Let it bubble for few seconds, then set aside.

Once the buns are baked, brush over the syrup and let them cool slightly before removing them from the tins. Enjoy them warm or at room temperature.

These are best enjoyed fresh, but any leftovers can be stored in an airtight container for 2–3 days. Just warm them in the microwave for 10 seconds before serving, as it makes them taste much better.

Choux pastry is my absolute favourite and is something my family loves. My kids ask for profiteroles for their birthdays and we make them every Christmas, too. This choux is flavoured with coffee and filled with coffee cream, as well as praline. The flavour is subtle but sublime and deepens with the chocolate sauce on top, finished with a further crunch of praline, making these an absolute treat.

Coffee cream profiteroles with chocolate

MAKES 22

FOR THE CHOUX

60g (2¼oz) unsalted butter, chopped

½ teaspoon salt

1 teaspoon caster sugar

125ml (4fl oz) water

1 teaspoon instant coffee granules

85g (3oz) plain flour

3 large eggs, lightly beaten

FOR THE PRALINE

a little vegetable oil

80g (2¾oz) caster sugar

4 teaspoons water

60g (2¼oz) hazelnuts

FOR THE FILLING

1 tablespoon instant coffee granules

1 tablespoon boiling water

400ml (14fl oz) double cream

150g (5½oz) mascarpone cheese

2 tablespoons caster sugar

FOR THE CHOCOLATE SAUCE

80g (2¾oz) caster sugar

80ml (2¾fl oz) water

200g (7oz) dark chocolate (70 per cent cocoa solids), roughly chopped

Put the butter, salt, sugar and measured water in a saucepan and bring to the boil, stirring to melt the butter and dissolve the sugar. Add the coffee and let it, too, dissolve. Reduce the heat to low, add the flour and stir continuously for a minute until the dough comes together and leaves the sides of the pan. Transfer this to a bowl and let it cool down slightly.

Meanwhile, preheat the oven to 180°C (350°F), Gas Mark 4. Line 2 baking sheets with nonstick baking paper and draw 22 x 4cm (1½ inch) circles on the paper. Flip the sheets over so the pencil marks are on the bottom but still visible through the paper.

Slowly add half the beaten egg to the dough and whisk with an electric whisk until well combined. Now add 1 tablespoon more egg and whisk again. You might not need the last bit of egg. The dough should be shiny and paste-like and fall from a spatula when lightly shaken. Put it in a piping bag with a 2cm (¾ inch) opening and pipe choux balls on the drawn circles. With a wet finger, pat out any peaks, then brush them all over with the leftover egg.

Bake for 30 minutes until golden. Remove them from the oven and prick the bottom of each choux ball with a skewer. Reduce the oven temperature to 160°C (325°F), Gas Mark 3 and bake for another 15 minutes until crispy and dried out. Set aside to cool.

continued overleaf

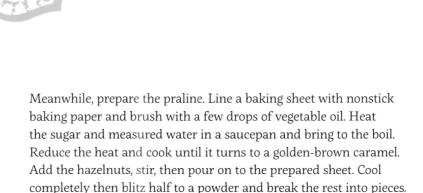

Meanwhile, prepare the praline. Line a baking sheet with nonstick baking paper and brush with a few drops of vegetable oil. Heat the sugar and measured water in a saucepan and bring to the boil. Reduce the heat and cook until it turns to a golden-brown caramel. Add the hazelnuts, stir, then pour on to the prepared sheet. Cool completely then blitz half to a powder and break the rest into pieces.

For the filling, mix the coffee and measured water until the coffee has dissolved, then let cool. Now whip the cream, mascarpone and sugar together until the mixture forms soft peaks. Add the cooled coffee mixture with 2 tablespoons of praline powder and fold it all in. Put this in a piping bag with a 2cm (¾ inch) opening.

For the sauce, heat the sugar and measured water in a saucepan. Bring to the boil, then reduce the heat to low and let it bubble for a minute. Remove from the heat and let it stand for another minute before pouring it over the chocolate in a heatproof bowl. Stir until melted. Put in a piping bag with a 1cm (½ inch) opening.

Cut each profiterole in half. Pipe the coffee cream in one half, then place the other half on top. Pipe on some chocolate sauce, top with a piece of praline, sprinkle with praline powder and serve.

You can prepare the choux buns 2–3 days in advance and keep them in an airtight container. If they go soft, just reheat them in the oven for 15 minutes. Once you fill them, serve immediately.

These little sponge fingers are as light as a feather and refreshing, with whipped cream and strawberries. Such a little treat. You can bake the sponge beforehand and just fill them with cream and strawberries – or other fruits – before serving.

Matcha and strawberry sponge fingers

MAKES 12

FOR THE SPONGE

2 large eggs, separated

70g (2½oz) caster sugar

50g (1¾oz) self-raising flour

20g (¾oz) cornflour

1 teaspoon matcha powder

20g (¾oz) unsalted butter, melted

FOR THE FILLING

250ml (9fl oz) double cream

2 tablespoons caster sugar

1 teaspoon vanilla extract

200g (7oz) strawberries, finely sliced

icing sugar, to serve (optional)

Preheat the oven to 180°C (350°F), Gas Mark 4. Line 2 baking sheets with nonstick baking paper. Draw 7cm (2¾ inch) lines on the paper, leaving enough space to spread in between. Turn the paper over so the pencil marks are on the bottom.

Put the egg whites in a bowl and whisk with an electric whisk until they form soft peaks. Now slowly add the sugar, 1 tablespoon at a time, whisking continuously until the mix is glossy and stiff. Now add the egg yolks and whisk for a few seconds until combined well.

Sift in the flour, cornflour and matcha powder and gently fold it all in. Next, add the melted butter and carefully fold it in, making sure to not lose too much air. Transfer to a piping bag, then place in the refrigerator for 30 minutes to set slightly.

Pipe the sponge fingers on to the lined sheets, over your drawn lines. Bake for 12–14 minutes until golden and dried out. Leave on the sheets for 5 minutes, then carefully transfer to a wire rack to cool.

Prepare the filling when you are ready to serve. Whip the cream, sugar and vanilla in a bowl until the mixture forms soft peaks. Transfer to a piping bag.

Place a sponge finger on a work surface, pipe over the cream and arrange some strawberries on top. Cover with another sponge finger. Repeat to sandwich together all the sponge fingers. Sprinkle icing sugar on top, if liked, and serve immediately.

Scones are one of the easiest things to bake and these are a bit special. The addition of chocolate with a subtle coffee hint gives them a slight richness. Delicious served warm with cream and jam.

Chocolate-coffee scones

MAKES 8–10

FOR THE SCONES

350g (12oz) self-raising flour, plus more for dusting

1 teaspoon baking powder

pinch of fine sea salt

90g (3¼oz) unsalted butter, chilled and chopped into small cubes

60g (2¼oz) caster sugar

20g (¾oz) cocoa powder

50g (1¾oz) dark chocolate chips

1 tablespoon instant coffee powder

1 tablespoon boiling water

110ml (3¾fl oz) buttermilk

1 egg, lightly beaten

TO SERVE

raspberry jam

clotted cream

Preheat the oven to 220°C (425°F), Gas Mark 7. Line a baking tray with nonstick baking paper and put the tray in the oven to heat up while you prepare the scones.

Mix the flour, baking powder and salt in a bowl. Add the butter and rub it into the flour with your fingers until you have a crumb texture, then stir in the sugar and cocoa powder and finally the chocolate chips.

In a separate bowl, mix the coffee and measured boiling water and stir until dissolved, then add the buttermilk and combine it well. Add this to the flour bowl and mix it all in with a fork.

Now place the dough on a floured work surface and bring it together, but don't knead too much. Once it comes together, flatten it to about 4cm (1½ inches) thick. Now take a 5cm (2 inch) round cutter and dip it into some flour. Press it on to the dough and cut out the scones. Next, press together what is left of the dough and cut out more scones.

Place the scones on the hot baking tray and brush the tops with the beaten egg. Bake for 10 minutes until risen. Since this dough has cocoa powder it's hard to tell when they are golden, so just check by pressing if they are cooked after 10 minutes. They should feel firm.

Enjoy them warm with jam and clotted cream, or if that's not possible, eat them within a day.

These are such a lovely little dessert and everyone gets their own individual meringue cake to enjoy. The cream is flavoured with salted caramel and finished with roasted hazelnuts for crunch, though you can roll these in other chopped nuts if you prefer, or even crushed-up biscuits or shaved chocolate.

Mini caramel and hazelnut meringue cakes

MAKES 20

4 egg whites

200g (7oz) caster sugar

1 teaspoon cornflour

600ml (20fl oz) double cream

4 tablespoons Salted caramel sauce (see page 189)

200g (7oz) roasted, chopped hazelnuts

Preheat the oven to 120°C (250°F), Gas Mark ½. Line 2 baking sheets with nonstick baking paper and draw 20 x 5cm (2 inch) circles on each sheet. Turn the paper over so the pencil marks are on the bottom but still visible through the paper.

In a clean bowl, whisk the egg whites with an electric whisk until they form soft peaks. Next, add the caster sugar, 1 tablespoon at a time, while continuing to whisk. Once it is glossy, add the cornflour and whisk for another couple of minutes until the mix is stiff and shiny. Transfer to a piping bag and pipe it to fill the drawn circles to form meringue discs.

Bake for 1½ hours, then turn off the oven and leave the meringues in there for another hour. Set aside to cool completely.

When you are ready to eat, whip the cream to soft peaks, add the salted caramel sauce and mix well. Transfer one-third of the cream to a piping bag. Pipe cream on top of half the meringues. Place another meringue on top of each to make a sandwich.

Using a palette knife, cover the sides and top of each meringue cake with the remaining cream then place in the refrigerator for 5 minutes.

Sprinkle the meringue tops with hazelnuts and serve immediately.

You can prepare the meringues 2–3 days in advance and keep them in an airtight container. Once sandwiched, serve immediately.

These cookies are our favourites and the kids love making them on their own now. They sometimes don't bother making the ganache but instead use Nutella, Biscoff or peanut butter to stuff the cookies, so you can do the same, if you like. You can also make just the cookies without any filling, but, whatever you decide to do, we hope you enjoy them as much as we do.

Our favourite cookies

MAKES 20–22

FOR THE COOKIES

200g (7oz) unsalted butter, softened

100g (3½oz) dark soft brown sugar

100g (3½oz) caster sugar

1 teaspoon vanilla extract

1 large egg, lightly beaten

120g (4¼oz) self-raising flour

120g (4¼oz) strong white bread flour

½ teaspoon baking powder

200g (7oz) dark chocolate chips

¼ teaspoon salt

FOR THE GANACHE

150ml (5fl oz) double cream

150g (5½oz) dark chocolate (70 per cent cocoa solids), roughly chopped

Start with the ganache. Bring the cream to the boil in a small saucepan. Place the chocolate pieces in a heatproof bowl and pour over the cream. Stir until melted, then cover and put in the refrigerator to set slightly.

Line a plate or tray with nonstick baking paper. Scoop out a heaped teaspoon of the set ganache, roll into a ball and place it on the prepared plate or tray. Make 20–22 balls and put them in the freezer while you prepare the cookie dough.

Put the butter and both sugars in a bowl and beat with a wooden spoon until creamy and pale. Now add the vanilla and egg and mix it in. Next, add both the flours, the baking powder, chocolate chips and salt and fold it all in, bringing it together into a slightly sticky dough. Cover and let it rest for 15 minutes.

Preheat the oven to 180°C (350°F), Gas Mark 4. Line 2 baking sheets with nonstick baking paper. Take a portion of dough about the size of a lime and form it into a disc in the palm of your hand. Now put a frozen ganache ball in the middle and seal it with the dough. Place on a prepared sheet. Repeat to form all the cookies, keeping enough distance between each to allow them to spread while baking. Put the trays in the refrigerator for 10 minutes so they set slightly.

Bake for 15 minutes, then leave to cool on a wire rack.

These can be stored in an airtight container for 2–3 days but are best eaten fresh when slightly warm and gooey.

Something on the side

Lemon and passion
fruit curd

Salted caramel sauce

Raspberry cardamom
jam

Spiced tomato chutney

Roasted aubergine
chutney

Coriander chutney

Onion chutney

Very spicy apple
chutney

Chilli chutney

Jaggery and tamarind
raita

I love lemon curd, it can add that zing and sharpness to any bake without much effort. I like to experiment with different fruits in the curd and you will also find a mango and lime curd recipe in this book (see page 26). But this version has to be my favourite. The passion fruit is a great partner to lemon in this very simple recipe.

Lemon and passion fruit curd

MAKES 1 MEDIUM BOWLFUL

finely grated zest and juice of 3 lemons

3 passion fruits

200g (7oz) caster sugar

100g (3½oz) unsalted butter

4 egg yolks, plus 1 whole egg

Put the lemon zest and juice, the pulp of the passion fruits, sugar and butter in a saucepan and bring to the boil, continuing to cook until the butter has melted.

In a bowl, whisk the egg yolks and whole egg together. Slowly add this to the pan and cook over a low heat, whisking continuously for 8–10 minutes until thick.

Pass through a sieve into a bowl. Let it cool completely.

This can be stored in an airtight container in the refrigerator for 3–4 days.

A drizzle of salted caramel sauce can brighten up any dessert, be it cake, cheesecake, ice cream, cookies or more. This simple recipe can be made in advance for you to use when you like. You can also have a play with your own flavours: stunning vanilla, fragrant cardamom, warm cinnamon or even a hint of chilli. If you are going to add a flavour, do so when adding the salt and make this sauce your own.

Salted caramel sauce

MAKES 1 MEDIUM BOWLFUL

220g (7¾oz) caster sugar
80ml (2¾fl oz) water
160ml (5½fl oz) double cream
½ teaspoon sea salt flakes
1 tablespoon unsalted butter

Put the sugar and measured water in a saucepan and give it a stir to start with; after this make sure not to stir or shake the pan. Place it over a low heat and let it simmer until the sugar has caramelized, or reached "caramel point" on a cooking thermometer.

Take it off the heat and slowly add the cream, stirring continuously and taking care, as it will spit. Return it to the heat and let it simmer over a low heat for a minute.

Next, add the salt and butter and let it bubble for a few seconds. Take it off the heat and let it cool down before using it.

Store it in a jar or an airtight container in the refrigerator for up to a week.

I love a good raspberry jam and the beauty of homemade jam is that you can actually taste the fruit and not just the sugar. The lemon juice here adds freshness, while the cardamom is very subtle but very present. The colour of this jam is so bright and inviting that, whether you add it to your bakes or just dollop it on some warm toast, it's bound to put a smile on your face.

Raspberry cardamom jam

MAKES 1 JAR

500g (1lb 2oz) fresh raspberries
400g (14oz) jam sugar
juice of 1 lemon
1 teaspoon ground cardamom

Put a small ceramic plate in the freezer.

Put all the ingredients in a heavy-based saucepan and cook over a medium heat until the sugar has dissolved. Now reduce the heat and bubble over a medium heat for 18–20 minutes until it gets a bit thicker and sticky.

Put a drop of the jam on the chilled plate and push the jam with your finger. If the jam gets crinkly, it means it's ready. If the jam is not yet set, it will not form any crinkles, in which case cook for another minute and test it again.

Once done, transfer to a clean, hot sterilized jar (see below). Seal once cooled. Store in a cool dry place and use it within 4 weeks.

> To sterilize jars, wash jars and lids in hot soapy water, preheat the oven to 160°C (325°F), Gas Mark 3, place the jars upside down on a baking tray and put in the oven for 20 minutes to dry. Meanwhile, boil a kettle and submerge the lids in boiling water in a bowl.

There are so many variations of tomato chutney in Indian cuisine, every region has its own version. You can call this mine, as it's the one I make often when I have plenty of tomatoes. It's got a little heat from chilli powder and a pinch of sweetness from sugar just to balance the sourness of the tomatoes. With no other spices, this truly is a chutney that highlights the glorious tomato.

Spiced tomato chutney

MAKES 1 MEDIUM BOWLFUL

3 tablespoons rapeseed oil

1 teaspoon nigella seeds

6 garlic cloves, finely chopped

2.5cm (1 inch) fresh root ginger, finely chopped

1 medium-sized onion, finely chopped

500g (1lb 2oz) tomatoes, finely chopped

1 teaspoon salt

1 teaspoon chilli powder

2 teaspoons caster sugar

Heat the oil in a pan and add the nigella seeds. When they start to sizzle, add the garlic and ginger and cook for 2 minutes until they start to colour lightly.

Add the onion and cook for 5 minutes until it softens.

Next, add the tomatoes, salt, chilli powder and sugar and cook over a medium-low heat for 15–20 minutes, stirring every now and then. The chutney should be broken down and have dried out slightly. Let it cool before serving.

Store it in an airtight container in the refrigerator for 6–8 days.

Roasting the aubergine not only makes it soft, it always adds that slight smokiness, too; that is what I am trying to bottle in this recipe. With my favourite garlic and chillies, this chutney forms such a great side for any savoury bakes. Or just spread some on a piece of toast, sprinkle some cheese on top and put under a hot grill for a minute. You will thank me for it.

Roasted aubergine chutney

MAKES 1 MEDIUM BOWLFUL

2 aubergines

2 tablespoons rapeseed oil, plus more for brushing

2 red chillies, finely chopped

4 garlic cloves, finely grated

½ teaspoon salt

1 teaspoon ground cumin

20g (¾oz) flat-leaf parsley, finely chopped

1 tablespoon lemon juice

Preheat a grill to medium and prick the aubergines with a knife all over. Brush some oil on them and place them on a baking tray. Roast under the hot grill for 30 minutes, turning them halfway through, until the skins are all charred and the insides are all mushy. Set aside until cool enough to handle.

Peel off the aubergine skins and discard, then mash or chop the flesh until it's all squashed.

Heat the oil in a pan, add the chillies and garlic and cook for 1 minute over a low heat until the garlic is just beginning to change colour. Then add the salt, cumin and parsley and mix well. Next, add the aubergine, increase the heat to high and cook for 2 minutes, stirring continuously. Take it off the heat, add the lemon juice and let cool.

You can serve this chutney warm or chilled, and it can be stored in an airtight container in the refrigerator for 3–4 days.

Finding this in my book should not come as a surprise, as I love a good coriander chutney. I think it is one of the best chutneys to come out of any Indian kitchen. My previous coriander chutney recipes are just put in a blender and blitzed, but this one is cooked, with a base of lentils, ginger and garlic and a few more things that marry well together. It makes for an absolutely delicious chutney.

Coriander chutney

MAKES 1 MEDIUM BOWLFUL

2 tablespoons rapeseed oil

1 tablespoon urad dal

1 tablespoon chana dal

2 dried red chillies

10 fresh curry leaves

6 garlic cloves, roughly chopped

2.5cm (1 inch) fresh root ginger, roughly chopped

1 banana shallot, chopped

1 teaspoon caster sugar

½ teaspoon salt

juice of 1 lime

60g (2¼oz) fresh coriander leaves, roughly chopped

Heat the oil in a saucepan, add the urad dal and chana dal with the dried red chillies and let it sizzle for a few seconds. Add 2 tablespoons of water, cover and cook over a low heat for 5 minutes.

Next, add the curry leaves, garlic, ginger and shallot and mix well. Cook over a high heat for 1 minute, then cover, reduce the heat to low and cook for 5 minutes.

Add the sugar and salt and mix well. Take the saucepan off the heat, add the lime juice and coriander leaves and mix well. Let it cool, then blitz it to a paste with 2 ice cubes and serve.

Store in an airtight container in the refrigerator for 2–3 days.

The sweetness of the onions, combined with a slight nuttiness from the groundnut oil, heat from the chillies and a hint of sourness from tamarind makes this a great all-rounder to enjoy with your bakes.

Onion chutney

MAKES 1 MEDIUM BOWLFUL

4 tablespoons groundnut oil
8 dried red chillies
6 medium-sized onions, roughly chopped
10 garlic cloves, roughly chopped
1 teaspoon tamarind paste
½ teaspoon salt
8 fresh curry leaves

Heat 3 tablespoons of the oil in a saute pan and add 6 of the red chillies and the onions. Cook over a medium-low heat for 10 minutes or until golden. Add the garlic, reduce the heat to low and cook for another 5 minutes.

Mix in the tamarind and salt. Let it cool slightly, then blitz to a rough paste and transfer to a bowl.

In a small saucepan, heat the remaining oil, add the remaining chillies with the curry leaves and let them sizzle. Pour over the onion chutney and serve.

Store in an airtight container in the refrigerator for 6–8 days.

This sour, slightly sweet, very spicy chutney is delightful with bakes, cheeses, curries, rice and flatbreads. It has layers of flavours from the ginger, garlic and chillies, sharp vinegar and ends with a slight sweet finish.

Very spicy apple chutney

MAKES 1 MEDIUM BOWLFUL

3 Bramley apples, peeled, cored and roughly chopped
1 medium-sized onion, finely chopped
100g (3½oz) fresh root ginger, peeled and finely chopped
10 garlic cloves, finely chopped
2 tablespoons chilli flakes
200ml (7fl oz) apple cider vinegar
200g (7oz) caster sugar
1 tablespoon salt

Put the apples, onion, ginger, garlic, chilli flakes and vinegar in a saucepan and cook over a low heat, uncovered, for 40–45 minutes until softened and dry. Stir regularly to ensure it is not catching.

Add the sugar and salt and cook for another 15–20 minutes, again stirring regularly, until dry and all cooked through. Let cool before serving.

Store in a jar or an airtight container in the refrigerator for 8–10 days.

Not for the faint-hearted, this chutney will definitely liven all your senses with its very punchy flavour. Not only is it super-spicy, depending on the variety of dried chilli you use, it also has a gentle sweetness in the background, while the garlic adds depth. Best of all, it's a very simple chutney to make.

Chilli chutney

MAKES 1 JAR

20 dried chillies (I use Kashmiri chillies)

6 tablespoons rapeseed oil

1 teaspoon cumin seeds

2 teaspoons coriander seeds

10 garlic cloves, roughly chopped

100ml (3½oz) water

½ teaspoon salt

3 tablespoons jaggery

Soak the chillies in a bowl of warm water for 30 minutes.

Heat half the oil in a saucepan, add the cumin and coriander seeds and let them sizzle for a few seconds. Next, add the garlic and cook over a low heat for 5 minutes until lightly golden. Drain the chillies, add them to the pan and cook for another 5 minutes, again over a low heat. Set aside to cool slightly.

Pour in the measured water and blitz to a paste with a hand blender, or in a micro chopper.

Heat the remaining oil in the same pan, add the paste and cook for 8–10 minutes until the oil starts to separate and the mixture dries out slightly.

Next, add the salt and jaggery and cook for a minute until the jaggery dissolves and cooks.

Transfer to a sterilized jar (see note on page 192 for how to sterilize jars) and seal once cooled. Store in the refrigerator and use within 4 weeks.

This might sound unusual, but I promise you will be pleasantly surprised because this simple-looking raita is a flavour explosion... and I don't say that lightly. The sour tamarind with the sweet jaggery and hot chillies, the spices and then cooling yogurt to bring it all together: definitely one to try. If you can't get hold of jaggery, use dark soft brown sugar instead.

Jaggery and tamarind raita

MAKES 1 MEDIUM BOWLFUL

2 tablespoons rapeseed oil

1 teaspoon black mustard seeds

1 teaspoon fennel seeds

10 fresh curry leaves

2 dried red chillies, broken up

1 tablespoon tamarind paste

50g (1¾oz) jaggery, cut into small pieces

¼ teaspoon salt

¼ teaspoon ground cinnamon

½ teaspoon ground ginger

250g (9oz) natural yogurt

Heat the oil in a pan and add the mustard seeds. Once they start to sizzle, add the fennel seeds, curry leaves and chillies and stir for a few seconds. Next, add the tamarind and jaggery and cook over a low heat until the jaggery has melted and the mix turns darker in colour, making sure to stir the whole time. Add the salt and spices and mix well.

Take it off the heat, add the yogurt and just swirl together. Transfer to a serving bowl.

This can be stored in the refrigerator for 2–3 days.

Index

Glossary of terms UK – US

Aubergine – eggplant

Baking paper – baking parchment

Baking tray – baking sheet

Baking sheet – cookie sheet

Bicarbonate of soda – baking soda

Bramley apples – cookers

Cake tin – cake pan

Caster sugar – superfine sugar

Chana dal – split and hulled brown chickpeas

Cider vinegar – apple cider vinegar

Clingfilm – plastic wrap

Coriander – cilantro

Cornflour – cornstarch

Courgette – zucchini

Dessicated coconut – dry unsweetened coconut

Digestive biscuits – graham crackers

Double cream – heavy cream

Flaked almonds – slivered almonds/sliced almonds

Golden caster sugar – unrefined superfine sugar

Grill – broiler/broil

Ground almonds – almond flour/almond meal

Icing sugar – confectioner's sugar

Massor dal – brown lentils

Plain flour – all-purpose flour

Self-raising flour – self-rising flour

Spring onions – scallions

Tomato purée – tomato paste

Urad dal – split black gram

Acknowledgements

With many thanks to:

My parents, Manju and Gulshan, for always being my inspiration in life.

My sisters, Niti and Alpa, for keeping it real for me, always.

My nephew and nieces, Vanshaj, Aashvi, Reet and Reva, for making me work hard so that I can inspire them one day.

My editor, Eleanor, for always having faith in my ideas and recipes, for being so patient and understanding, and for always being there for me.

Juliette, for working so hard on the design of the book.

Polly and Lucy, for their work on fine-tuning the text.

My photographer, Nassima, who understands my vision and creates such magic with her camera to show my food in its best glory.

Emily, my food stylist, who is simply the best and understands my food better than anyone.

My lovely friends, who always help me with their love, support and feedback on my bakes.

To the most important people in my life, my kids, Sia and Yuv. Their constant feedback, criticism of my bakes, joy when they love a recipe, honesty when they don't... They are the best in-house team I could ever ask for. It would not be possible to do what I do without their love and support.

And the most important person of all, my husband Gaurav, for always being there for me. From putting up with the kitchen being upside-down, to trying my experiments for dinner and eating the same bakes for days, I am grateful for his patience throughout.